An
Old Creed
for a
New Day

An
Old Creed
for a
New Day

by DANA PROM SMITH

FORTRESS PRESS   PHILADELPHIA

COPYRIGHT © 1975 BY FORTRESS PRESS

Library of Congress Catalog Card Number 74-26331

ISBN 0-8006-1093-8

4690A75   Printed in U.S.A.   1-1093

For Paul, Timothy, and Elizabeth,

"tutors unto Christ"

Contents

Preface

People affiliate with religious groups for three reasons: to seek salvation, to find meaning, to enjoy fellowship. In American churches one often finds the conservatives offering salvation, the liberals looking for meaning, and *everyone* claiming to be the friendliest church in town.

Salvation, meaning, and fellowship all represent legitimate human needs. Salvation is the restoration of a relationship with the God and Father of our Lord Jesus Christ. Since life is filled with vicissitudes and uncertainties, a sure and certain sense of ultimate salvation can give a person a rock on which to stand. A search for meaning is an attempt to make sense out of the apparent absurdity of life. While salvation involves one on a personal and emotional level, the search for meaning is an intellectual pursuit. To enjoy fellowship is such a basic human need that many people will sell their souls for it. They will endure the ludicrous requirements of college fraternities and sororities, pay exorbitant fees at country clubs, smoke pot and shoot acid, and participate in sexually degrading practices just to be part of the "in group."

A person's religious experience generally revolves around the pursuit of salvation, meaning, and fellowship. In an authentic experience all three are present. The Lord's Supper of the Christian faith is a case in point. It is a means by which a person becomes vividly aware of his personal relationship with God, that is, his salvation. It is a means of seeing through the apparent absurdity of life by focusing on the suffering of Christ. It is a means of fellowship as believers share the wine and the bread.

The Apostles' Creed is another example. Too often the Creed is simply an archaic statement that is mumbled or chanted without understanding, whereas its purpose is to *explain* the salvation wrought in Jesus Christ and to help a believer understand himself in the light of that salvation. The Creed is not a means of salvation; it assumes salvation. In the fellowship of the church, the Creed helps us to understand the meaning of salvation for our lives. It covers the whole range of Christian understanding and serves as a brief theological or doctrinal statement which guides a believer's reflection on the meaning of what has been experienced in faith.

This small volume is a slice of one believer's life as he works out his own salvation in fear and trembling. It is far from final because a person struggles with and tries to understand the meaning of his faith through all the stages of his life, even to his death.

1

I Believe In

Several years ago a prominent member of the Saudi Arabian royal family visited the United States for medical treatment. As a part of diplomatic courtesy the Department of State arranged for him to attend a concert of the New York Philharmonic. When he was asked what part of the concert he liked best, he replied, "the first part, before the man with the stick came in." He was, of course, referring to the tune-up time with its scratchy, grating, squeaky cacophony. One's point of view depends entirely on where one stands.

The Apostles' Creed begins with a simple assertion about man's stance: "I believe in." If in reading or repeating the Creed we forget the crucial preposition "in," we may well miss the whole point. For the focus of the Creed is not on the content of a man's *mind*, but on what he does with his *life*.

When the Lord God confronted the man and the woman in the Garden of Eden after they had disobeyed him, he did not ask them who they were or what they thought, but where they were standing. It was the appropriate question because they were in hiding. They had hid themselves because they were

1

afraid. In their fear they were standing by themselves, isolated, unrelated to anything else.

But standing does not mean standing alone. It means standing in *relation* to something or someone else. When we forget this and try to stand alone, we may end up not standing at all. The preposition "in" at the very beginning of the Creed ties the creedal faith and affirmations to God and changes "belief" from a proposition to a relationship.

Some people think the Creed is a series of theological statements about God, man, and the world—an acknowledgement that God exists plus a series of statements about his nature. If it were, then the Creed should read, "I believe *that* God is the Almighty Father who created the heavens and the earth." Now, while that may be an accurate theological statement, it is not the intent of the Creed.

The phrase "I believe *in*" removes the Creed from the category of statements about God and makes it an affirmation of God's relationship to man. The faith expressed in the language of the Creed is one that involves standing in relationship to God.

Too often theology has been understood as a speculative attempt to understand the nature of God, forgetting Saint Paul's insight that man sees even himself—not to speak of God—"through a glass darkly." Theology is the attempt to look at one's life in relationship to God, to see oneself in terms of one's stance as a believer in Jesus Christ. Either theology serves as an illuminator of human life or it fails in its purpose. And if it succeeds in illuminating, that theology is a reflection of the relationship God has given man in Jesus Christ.

2

The Creed begins with the affirmation that theological doctrine is *not* the heart of the Christian experience. When it says "I believe *in*," it points away from itself to the experience of God's presence and the reality of the relationship to God in Jesus Christ. The Creed is not an abstract speculation about eternal verities. It is reflection on the meaning of a life lived in the light of God's grace.

When one person believes in another he goes beyond the limits of his mind. When a couple approach marriage, they almost always do it with high anticipation and nagging doubts, for they are being compelled by their human needs to take a step beyond what they know. No one ever knows enough about another to marry that person; they have had glimpses and hints, of course, but there is not that sure and certain knowledge which is required if the basis of the marriage is knowledge. So they proceed on faith.

People are forever contrasting faith and knowledge as if the two were opposites. Actually, they depend on each other. A man does not gather every piece of knowledge obtainable and then make his decisions. If that were his approach, he would never make a decision because he would never know enough. His faith takes him out beyond the limits of his knowledge and affords him the possibility of new experiences, and thus of new knowledge. Faith's movement forward and outward is called "growing in grace."

Christopher Columbus had some knowledge to support his belief that the world was not flat, and on the basis of what he knew he went beyond what he knew and discovered a whole new world. Had he stayed within the bounds of his knowledge, he would have remained an Italian sailor plying his trade within sight of Portugal. Columbus based his journey on his limited knowledge and abiding faith; the Creed speaks of a journey based on an experience of grace and on an abiding faith that beyond that experience is a gracious reality. Columbus ventured forth with a faith derived from his experience of things; a believer ventures forth with a faith derived from an experience of grace. Columbus believed *that* the world was round; the believer believes *in* God. The first is an impersonal knowledge, the second a personal one in which knowledge and faith are even more intimately tied. Indeed, when the Old Testament speaks of sexual experience, one of the highest experiences of grace, it uses the word "know."

A person begins to know himself only by his relationships. Modern man often forgets this and thinks that he knows himself by his accomplishments, thereby assuming that he stands alone. The Creed begins with the assumption that a man can understand himself as a human being only in terms of his relationships. It asserts that man stands in relationship to God.

Modern man usually identifies himself by citing a variety of accomplishments. When a typical American male is asked about himself, he will invariably reply with a description of his job. After awhile he may bring out pictures of his wife and children, but he will seldom if ever speak about his parents, brothers, aunts, and uncles. In modern society, knowledge is an accomplishment. In a commercial society which values marketable skills, "know-how" is an accomplishment.

Ironically, for many believers the "believe" in "I

4

believe in" refers to an intellectual accomplishment, as if to say that a creedal statement is a means of proving one is a Christian. The baleful result of this confusion is to make abstract that which is concrete, and impersonal that which is personal. A relationship is made into a transaction.

The aim of the Creed is to deny this confusion by the use of "in." The believer looks at his life and tries to understand it in terms of his relationship with God, not in terms of his own accomplishments. Thus the Creed is not so much a collection of statements about God as a series of affirmations about man's perceptions of the meaning of his relationship with God.

In addition to that, the phrase "I believe in" speaks of the quality of the relationship. In an age which thinks a great deal about the ability of people to "relate" to each other, the Creed drives home the point that relating is not the heart of the Christian faith. Faith and trust are, and they are unique forms of relationship. They point beyond the one relating to the One being related *to*. They move away from the one believing to the One believed *in*.

A man cannot live well if he does not have something for which he is willing to die, for the substance of his life comes from that to which he has given his life. In an age of abstractions, modern man may think that one can give his life to ideas, policies, and programs. Freedom, democracy, and self-determination are causes that claim fealty. They may lay claim to man's sacrifices and sustain him. But they all fail because they cannot respond to the commitment they demand.

A man cannot long give his life to ideals, because he will inevitably and eventually get used up. The ideals cannot respond to his faith with love and mercy, for they have none. About the only thing commitment to ideals can give a man is self-righteousness. His commitment is his achievement. The phrase "I believe in" moves beyond the "I," through the "believe in," right on to God—for belief in terms of faith and trust is not an achievement but a response to a gift. It takes place not so much at the initiative of man as in response to God's achievement in Jesus Christ.

The difference between commitment to ideals and faith in God is the distinction between an achievement of goodness and an elicitation of faith. A child believes in his parents because of their gestures of love toward him. He is unaware of himself as he is caught up in his response to them. Commitment is self-conscious in its avowal of its ideals and thus always tainted by self-righteousness. The Creed does not speak of the so-called committed Christian. It speaks of a person absorbed in his experience of grace in Jesus Christ.

Experience by itself is not enough, for a man must *think* about what has happened to him and what he has done to others. In addition to illuminating the meaning of one's experiences, the Creed serves to guide experiences. Plato once observed in his *Apology* that the unexamined life is not worth living.

While the Creed is not a collection of statements about God, man, and the world, it *is* about the nature of the relationship God has established with man. Oddly enough, the Creed is not a collection of human ideas about God. Rather, it contains divine ideas about man. It is about man seen from the divine perspective. As such, it serves as a guide for the self-examined life, a life examined by the self, not in terms of the self, but in terms of God's message.

Some people believe that because the Bible uses human images for God that it is really a book about man's ideas of God. The images, though, are expressions rather than conceptions—expressions pointing to the quality of the relationship between God and man. The Creed serves man as a guide in self-understanding and self-examination.

The Creed begins with a personal affirmation of faith in God, and thus it speaks about the nature of the Christian life. What it sets forth is not a series of ideas, emotions, or morals but an experience of relationship with God in Jesus Christ. The Creed serves not so much to give us final and complete answers as to provoke us to reflect upon our experiences and examine them.

An unexamined life is liable to illusion, and when the illusion suffers, one becomes, obviously, disillusioned. Illusion and disillusion are familiar to modern man. People have given themselves to causes and lived by their commitments only to find them illusions. It is not enough just to reflect on one's experiences. There must be guides.

Careful thinking requires two things: the data with which to think and the norms by which to think. For the believer, the data of his reflection is his experience of God's graciousness; the norm is God's Word.

The Creed begins with a statement of the data, "I believe in," and then proceeds to the norms by which a man reflects on his experience of faith and grace. The norms are the qualities of the relationship God has with him in Jesus Christ. The Creed, then, expresses not so much what *man* thinks about *God* as what meaning man finds for his life when he reflects on his life in the light of what *God* thinks about *him*.

The hoped for result of such reflection is a life of integrity, a life that is purposefully whole. At a time when the call to relevancy rings in the ears, it is crucial to call to mind the importance of integrity. Every man faces a twin challenge in life: to be faithful to himself and to be in contact with the world around him. If he chooses relevancy and forgets integrity, as much of modern society seems to do, he will end up simply being a pale reflection of his environment. If he chooses integrity without a concern for pertinence, then he will end up in isolated splendor, firmly rooted in the past but remaining right where he has always been, and with spiritual rigor mortis setting in. The first is limp, and the second is brittle.

The function of the Creed is to allow the reflection to take place in terms of both integrity and relevancy. To believe in God is not only to see oneself in relation to him, but also to see oneself in relation to the world He has made. One of the fallacies of looking at the Creed as a series of finally true theological propositions rather than as an affirmation of the relationship of trust is that it gradually leads a person down the road of integrity without pertinence. A person gets hooked on theological formulations of the past.

Archbishop William Temple once observed that one of the beneficial results of the Christian faith is the ability it gives a person to see life steadily and to see it whole. That is the function of the Creed. It is not a matter of indoctrination, putting neatly packaged ideas into the heads of believers. It is rather an education, a leading forth into fresh understanding of one's life in the light of the gospel of Jesus Christ.

2

God

"Getting it together" is a common contemporary pastime. It betrays the fragmentation of our times. Just as a thirsty man wants water, so a fragmented man seeks integrity. He wants to make sense out of his life by seeing it whole. He is not content with having bits and pieces of his life lying around before him, and, although he is often overwhelmed by diversity and disunity, he still needs to get it together.

There have been two responses to this fragmentation. One has been a flat, stale, and unprofitable sameness in which all the diversity has been forced into a single mold. It is an attempt to achieve unity through uniformity. In the story of Procrustes' bed, out of Greek mythology, a highwayman with a nasty preference for uniformity forced every passerby to lie on his bed. If the person was too short, he stretched him out; if too long, he cut him down to size. Everyone had to fit. The Procrustean bed survives today in men's attempts to achieve unity through uniformity at the cost of lopping off a good bit of the diversity of life and stretching other things way out of proportion.

Another response to fragmentation involves abandoning the quest for wholeness altogether. Rather than try to achieve a unity, it capitulates to the piecemeal; it accepts divisions without question. As a person tramps from one medical specialist to another, he never bothers to wonder if there is not someone in the clinic who can bring it all together. Fragmentation, the gift of specialization, becomes the order of the day.

Christian theology is a reflection on both the integrity and the diversity of human experience. It is an attempt to appreciate simultaneously its variety and wholeness. It assumes that all the bits and pieces can be put together so that there is neither a stale uniformity nor a debilitating fragmentation.

There are three possible ways of looking at the richness and variety of religious experience. One way is to dismiss it because it doesn't fit the Procrustean bed. Another is to assume that the experiences are so complex and contradictory that there must be several gods. "I'll worship my god and you worship yours" runs the familiar polytheistic refrain. The third way is to believe that there is one God revealing himself in diverse ways.

The Christian begins with the belief that God is one and single, yet many and complex. While he may be one, he reveals himself in different ways. The doctrine of the Trinity—expressed in the tripartite division of the Apostles' Creed—is an attempt to understand the varieties of religious experience while believing in one God. It says little about God himself, but sets the terms for a person's understanding of the varied relationships he has with God.

Martin Luther referred to God as the *deus absconditus*, the hidden God. John Calvin said that man could know the attributes of God, but not God as he is known to himself. Paul called God a mystery, which is a way of saying that he is beyond our knowledge. These comments recognize that most of the words used for God say nothing about him. Words like "infinite," "eternal," and "unchangeable" sound good until one realizes that human beings never experience limitlessness, timelessness, and unchangeableness. Since people do not experience them, we have no knowledge of them. Such words are really statements about the limitations of man's knowledge and experience. As exercises in humility they are great, but they are not very useful in talking about God.

Other words come from human experience and seem at first to say something about God, but they too are really about his relationship to man. If a boy calls a man his father, he is not saying so much about the man as he is about his relationship to the man. If he goes on to say that his father is a "great guy," he is still talking about the way his father relates to him. When John wrote that God is love, he was not defining God; he was talking about his experience of God in Jesus Christ.

The doctrine of the Trinity, then, is not a statement about the nature of God. It refers instead to a person's varied experiences of God. Ironically, since theology is not really about God but about man's relationship to God, the Trinity is ultimately about the various ways a man looks at himself in the light of God's grace.

Briefly stated, the doctrine of the Trinity says that the God who created the world enfleshed himself in a particular man, and after that man was crucified, rose, and ascended, he continued to abide among men. The traditional words used to identify these three experiences of God are God the Father, God the Son, and God the Holy Spirit.

Part of the problem is that much conventional language about God inadequately expresses the conviction that the unifying presence of God lies behind the variety of religious experiences. The doctrine of the Trinity is an attempt to find a verbal framework in which a man may fruitfully understand the diverse ways God encounters him. His experiences of awe and comfort, enlightenment and obscurity, doubt and faith, fear and reassurance are part of the warp and woof of the cloth from which the concept of the Trinity is woven.

Historically, the doctrine of the Trinity did not arrive one fine day as a full-blown communication directly from the lips of God himself. It developed as believers struggled with the meaning of their experiences. At first, there was probably a binity, two Persons, the Father and the Son, rather than a Trinity. Paul said: "For us there is one God, the Father, from whom are all things and for whom we exist, and one Lord, Jesus Christ, through whom are all things and through whom we exist." (1 Cor. 8:6-7)

The earliest Christians believed that God had revealed himself in Jesus Christ. Jesus was more to them than just another spokesman for God, like the Old Testament prophets. There was an unusual authenticity to his presence. Because of this and because of his resurrection from the dead, they believed that he was the enfleshment of the God whom their fathers had worshiped. As time passed, they also became aware that his presence continued to abide with them in their community, although he was no longer physically present.

Upon reflection, these early Christians found that God had encountered them in three different ways, each of the ways being different enough to force them to think about their relationship to God in new terms. The old, simple monotheism of their fathers was not enough. The word "God" by itself was simply not diverse enough to contain the variety of their experiences. They had grown beyond the intellectual limits of their vocabularies and were no longer able to adequately express what had happened to them. This realization led to the development of the language of the Trinity.

Now, in some ways their language is obsolete today, for it was cast in a philosophical and psychological framework quite foreign to a modern believer. In order to explain the unity of man's experience of God, the early Christians used the words "substance" and "essence," and this substance or essence was equally present in all three "Persons" of the Trinity. The multiplicity of their experiences led them to the word "Person." It is important for us to realize that the word "Person" does not mean a self-conscious and identifiable individual. The fathers of the church were driving at distinctiveness, not isolation and separation. The three Persons of the Trinity possessed the same essence or substance and yet were expressed in distinct modes.

One of the early theologians of the church tried to compare the Persons of the Trinity with three different men, Peter, James, and John. Their common humanity was their unity, but they were still distinct persons. This analogy was unacceptable because it verged on polytheism.

A little more satisfactory, but still suffering the infirmities of all analogies, was the comparison to one man's having three distinctive roles in his span of life:

a son to his own father, a husband to his own wife, and a father to his own children. These three primary relationships corresponded to his other relationships; that is, he was filial, companionable, and fatherly to other people depending upon the nature of the relationship. The man was a single, not a split, personality, and yet he had three distinctive primary relationships. He was fully *in* each relationship, and yet each relationship was unique.

One of the liabilities of the language about the Trinity used by the early church was that it caused people to think that they were talking about the nature of God when, in fact, they were merely talking about their perceptions of their relationship with God. The sad result of this confusion has been that a doctrine which was originally designed to allow diversity came to mean uniformity. Believers were thought to be damned or saved on the basis of their ability to master the subtleties of Platonic philosophy.

The doctrine of the Trinity is useful for the Christian if he remembers that it is a procedural doctrine rather than a substantial one; that is, it has to do with the way one goes about the task of thinking about the faith, rather than the nature of the faith itself.

The drive behind the development of the doctrine of the Trinity was the need to authenticate the Christian experience. Was the God whom they experienced as Judge also the one whom they experienced as Savior? Was the seemingly inaccessible God of the universe the same God they found abiding in their daily lives? Could a person experience wrath and mercy from the same God? The guide for that type of reflection was formulated in the doctrine of the Trinity which allows a diversity and affirms a unity.

14

A small boy is often bewildered by his mother. When he misbehaves, she punishes him; and when he cries under the punishment, she comforts him. When he tries to say he is sorry, she helps him find the words. She is his judge, his reconciler to his judge, and his friend during and after the punishment. Out of all this bewildering variety of relationships with his mother he often gets the message that, no matter how she is coming across, she is still the same loving mother. A Christian's experience of God parallels the little boy's experience of his mother. The doctrine of the Trinity is profoundly indigenous to human experience.

Some philosophies and religions try to make each person fit a prefabricated mold, and thus they have to stretch points and cut people down to size to make the fit possible. Other viewpoints on life seem haphazard with no fundamentally unifying outlook giving cohesion and integrity to a person's life. There should be a way to see all the variety and diversity while retaining a wholeness. The doctrine of the Trinity is a means to that end.

In an age of specialized fragmentation, the Trinity is not only a means of discourse; it is also a challenge to those who speak about integrity but live in bits and pieces and to those who try to jam their lives into some ideological straitjacket. It does not claim to unravel the mystery of God. It claims that there is a way to understand both the variety and unity of human experience and to see that variety and unity finally as an experience of God himself.

3

The Father Almighty

When a man calls God his Father, he supposedly assumes that God's fatherhood parallels human fatherhood. According to this line of reasoning God is like a human father, only writ large and perfect. By drawing such a comparison between God and man, people often think that they are saying something about God while, in fact, they are really saying something about themselves. When a man calls God his Father, he is also calling himself God's son.

A common theological mistake is made when one thinks he is defining God by calling him Father. God is not confined within the limits of human experience. A person has said nothing at all about God by picturing him as the ideal human father and then carrying that description to the absolute. All that has really been said is that the person claims a relationship with God akin to his relationship with his human father. Knowledge is built upon a comparison. When one speaks of electronic waves, he is drawing an analogy between electricity and oceans, but a person's knowledge of electricity does not stop at the water's edge.

The words used for God in the Bible are found in ordinary human discourse. "Shepherd," "father," and "husband" are obvious examples. "Spirit" originally meant "wind," and "God Almighty" literally meant "God of the mountains." However, the biblical writers also knew that these words never did justice to the matter, for God was beyond their experience. The words really reflected only their own experience.

While the language of faith arises out of the language of human experience, this does not mean that man's understanding of his relationship with God is merely the phantom of his desires. When God speaks to man, he uses the language of human experience, but it does not necessarily follow that man's experience is the judge of God's message. One does not take his conceptions of God's fatherhood and use them to define God's fatherhood. Rather he tries to grasp the meaning of his own experience of fatherhood and sonship in the light of God's relationship with him. His theology enlightens his experience. While the words used for man's relationship with God may be cut from the cloth of human life, the pattern has been given by God.

There are two types of knowledge, personal and impersonal. One may know something *about* someone else, and one may know *him*. When the question "Yes, but what is he really like?" is asked, the desire is to get beyond knowledge *about* someone to a knowledge of *him*. The first type of knowledge needs no relationship; the second type requires it. With the first there is no commitment; the second demands it. The first gives no insights into one's self; the second enables a man to see himself anew. When a man loves a woman, he sees himself in a new way; it is part of the ecstasy of love. When a woman becomes a mother, her life takes on a new dimension and she sees herself anew.

Often marriage is compared in the Bible with the relationship between God and man. One of the results of a good marriage is a constant growth in self-understanding. People do not gain insight into themselves apart from others. It is always in relationship, and the requirement of the relationship is a commitment in trust.

When the first part of the Creed begins "I believe in God the Father Almighty," this is not a statement about the existence of God. It is a statement about one's relationship to him, and as such, it raises the question of independence and self-sufficiency. One of the prevailing assumptions in modern western society is the desirability of independence. A belief in God immediately calls into question such assumptions and is, perhaps, one of the reasons why modern man has such a hard time believing in God.

In the story of the man and woman in the second and third chapters of Genesis the fundamental issue is man's desire for independence and sovereignty. Many have thought the real problem with the passage has been a reconciliation of science and religion, and as with many similar debates, the issue was falsely drawn. The story has nothing to do with how the world was made—that's a scientific question—for the story deals with the dilemma of man.

The pity of the confusion is that the story's great insights have been missed. The ancient Hebrew assumed that God made the world. His question was the origin of man's malaise, which was man's desire to live as if God were not. The serpent tempted the man at the point of his self-sufficiency: "Don't you want to be like God knowing good and evil?" The phrase "good and evil" did not mean a knowledge of right and wrong, it was not a question of morals. The phrase meant a knowledge of everything: "Don't you want to be like God knowing everything?" He was tempted at the point of his desire for independence. He wanted to be like God so that he could live as though God were not, for he rightly assumed that living in trust with God limited his freedom.

The temptation was to live without relationship, to substitute knowledge for faith. A great many marriages fail at this point. Indeed, a great many other relationships fail at this point, for a relationship requires trust. If a person requires proof of love, the relationship is destroyed. One person can never know enough about another to have all the doubts answered. At some point he must go beyond knowledge to a leap of faith, not because faith and knowledge are opposites, but because he recognizes that knowledge has its limits, and in the business of living a person must always go beyond what he knows. If he does not, he will lead a very limited and lonely life.

Ironically, the desire for a freedom based on knowledge is imprisoning, for if a man never goes beyond what he knows, he will never go anywhere. Faith leads beyond the limits of knowledge. If a person tries to know so that he can believe, he will neither know nor believe. If he believes so that he might know, then he may develop a knowledgeable faith.

The second and third chapters of Genesis are not creation narratives. They are parabolic stories of everyman, for by means of a delightfully intriguing story man is questioned about his desire to live without God. The atheism in the story is not a modern theoretical type. It is a practical atheism in which a man intellectually acknowledges a belief in a Supreme Being but decides to live as though God were *not,* which is where most men find themselves. There is also the odd possibility that some men live as though God *were*, but refuse to believe that he exists.

The story strikes at the heart of man's malaise, the malaise of living apart and alone. When a man says that he believes in God, he is putting a question to himself, a question about the substance of his life. He is calling into question his desire to live by what he knows and does, and making himself face once again the imperative for a relationship with God.

In confessing faith in God the Father Almighty, a person is saying not only that he believes in God, but that the God he believes in is his Father. Children understand themselves in relationship to their parents. If they believe the parents benevolent, it will affect the way they see themselves; they will likely think well of themselves. If they see the parents as indifferent, they will hold themselves in low esteem. If they think the parents hostile, they will likely disavow themselves.

One ought to be sensitive to the way people view their parents. Someone who cannot speak well of his parents probably devalues himself as well. Even if one cannot applaud all the parental foibles and idiosyncrasies, it is important to have a basically favorable attitude toward one's parents, for a person cannot hate his parents and love himself. They are his origin. Similarly, if a person believes that his Creator loves him, he will be more likely to love and value himself.

Much of life is spent in an anxiety about the attitudes of other people. A child interprets the wrath of a mother or father as either a justified indignation at some misdeeds or a personal rejection. He has to figure out what is basic in the relationship and what is peripheral. When a child runs away, he is generally greeted on his return with a mixture of anger and relief; and if the parents love the child, the anger is a product of the anxiety they felt for his welfare. Unfortunately, there are children who feel that their experiences of love are just interludes in a tale of indifference.

There is plenty of evidence that this is an unjust and cruel world. There is just as much evidence that it is an indifferent world. There is some evidence that it is a benevolent world. But is the benevolence a deceptive interlude or is it the fundamental reality? As with the little boy after a confusing afternoon with his mother, a person might wonder how to come to terms with the bewildering variety of experiences the world has to offer.

Quantitatively, there is probably more cruelty in the world than benevolence—at least more of it gets in the newspapers. The newspapers, however, print the unusual things, not the normal. One seldom sees banner headlines recounting the glories of a grandmother caring for her grandchildren during a mother's sickness. That is not extraordinary. One reads instead about child abandonment and molestation. Likewise, there are headlines when a baby is dumped on the doorstep of the local police precinct station, but at most only a birth notice when a loving family welcomes a new addition. An unexpected result of this unbalanced coverage is that the newspapers affirm that goodness is normal and wickedness abnormal.

While there may be more evil than good, man still persists in looking at evil as an aberration. Even such supposedly toughminded people as reporters make that assumption in the selection of news. Wars and turmoil crowd peace and tranquility off the front page, not because wars are what really count, but because they are extraordinary.

Moral ambiguity can be resolved in one of three ways. One can say that goodness is an aberration, that evil is an aberration, or that both evil and good are unreal and irrelevant distinctions. The first says the world is hostile, the second, benevolent, and the third, indifferent. The quality of a person's life will be decisively influenced by his choice of outlook. Each outlook requires that a person go beyond what he knows. Each outlook will affect the way he thinks about what he does know. One cannot escape the moral ambiguity of life. Therefore, one never knows enough to make a rational decision; one can only make a reasonable decision. And the decision will be a leap of faith.

One of the functions of doctrine is to discourage shoddy and ill-considered decisions and to make people think about the decisions they have made. The Creed is not only about the fact that one serves God, but also about the quality of that relationship. When the Creed affixes the word "Father" to the word "God," it is speaking of the quality of man's life. It is affirming that the relationship is benevolent.

The next word in the Creed is "Almighty." A good many people slide over that word unaware of its importance. It settles the issue of the primacy of goodness and benevolence in the world. An impotent goodness is not worth much, for there is not much point to a God who has failed.

The Creed asks the question about the power of benevolence. Facing the three possibilities of indifference, hostility, and benevolence, one has to make a choice. In some ways it is easier to lapse into a sense of hostility or indifference because of the abundance of evidence in their support. However, the difficulty with hostility is that one must then try to explain away the good and just and beautiful things of life. When a person is tempted to ask the question, "If God is so good, why does he allow all this evil and misery?" he might try reversing the question. Then he is faced not with the problems of pain, injustice, and hatred, but the questions of pleasure, justice, and love. Can one adequately explain the power of love by calling it an interlude in a life of indifference or an aberration from the norm (hatred)?

As difficult as it is for a person to believe in a benevolent God, it is far more difficult to believe that love and mercy are aberrations, absurdities, or interludes. Such a belief does not explain the experience of someone who has been loved wisely and well, and it is totally self-defeating for the person whose life has been misery. The words "Almighty Father" challenge the person groping toward a decision about the fundamental ambiguity of life.

However, if one believes that life is fundamentally good, then he must face honestly the fact that evil exists. Seeing life as fundamentally good is not necessarily self-deluding. As a matter of fact, it is a way of being realistic because it acknowledges the agony of life while at the same time seeing the original possibilities of mercy and love. The pain of betrayal can occur only after there has been trust in someone else. A person's heart is wrenched when he sees pictures of starving children in the newspapers because he has also seen happy and well-fed children playing in the yard. What could have been is part of the pain and agony of so much that is.

As one considers his experience, it becomes apparent that no matter how much grief and evil there is in the world and no matter how difficult it is to square that grief and evil with a belief in a gracious Father, believing in him is the only way to make sense out of what is going on in one's life. A couple going through the agony of a divorce can sweep it all aside with a casual wave of the hand and pretend that it is not really too important. However, they are deluding themselves if they do that. Even while experiencing anguish, the only way a person can treat his anguish with respect is to know that the pain is not right, that there could have been something else.

The poignancy of so much of life is evidence enough that the roots of human experience are in grace, mercy, and love. The recollections of lost friendships, children disappointing their parents, marriages gone sour, and jobs not living up to expectations are more than passing disappointments. They point to one of the bedrock assumptions of man's experience—that life is essentially good. His sense of the tragic and the poignant makes sense only in the light of an essential goodness. It is not enough to dismiss these deepest human experiences as mere projections of human desire, as some would have it. Although people often project outward their deepest needs, fears, and desires, one cannot convert that proposition into the belief that *all* the needs, fears, and desires of men are mere projections. That would be a logical fallacy.

The real issue is whether a person's beliefs help him to understand better his various experiences. It is a poor idea that reduces to illusion some of man's most profound experiences. The test of an idea or belief is its ability to interpret the deepest of human experiences and the widest range of them. It is a small idea which dismisses a multitude of experiences because they do not fit a preconceived mold. If that happens, it is not the experiences that should be called into question, but rather the idea. It is a shallow idea which is unable to cope with the depth of human experience. If an idea resists being explored in depth, it may not be worth considering.

The hopes and fears, the tragedies and triumphs, the pains and pleasures, and the poignancies of life are simply not adequately understood if they are based on a belief that the final reality of life is hostile or indifferent. Man is more than an indifferent brute or a cowering beast. He has dreams and visions, debaucheries and failures. The dreams and visions can be understood only in the light of a God who is an Almighty Father, and the debaucheries and failures are best understood as negations of an essential goodness.

The Creed is designed to help a person gain deeper insight into his life, not to tell him what to believe; it is the handmaiden of insight. Man's freedom comes from his ability to understand himself in relationship to God. This is what allows him to see his potential; he not only knows what he *is* but what he can be.

There is a cynical statement which is nevertheless pertinent: "It's not so much what you know as who you know." The Creed is a reflection on Whom the believer knows, because what he knows is a product of Whom he knows—that is, his life and his accomplishments are seen in light of his relationship to one God who is his Almighty Father. In the midst of an ambiguous life he sees himself as the son of a loving God.

4

Maker of heaven and earth

Several questions can be asked about every event. Some people have an interest in personalities and want to know who was involved. Others have an interest in the facts and want to know what happened. Others have a mechanical interest and want to know how it happened. Still others search out the meaning of an event; they want to know why it happened. All four considerations are valid and important, but each one, by itself, does not make much sense. They all require each other for the full picture.

The questions of how and why are often thought to be at war with each other, for one is a scientific question and the other is a religious question. Science asks how things take place and religion asks why. Now, everyone is part scientist and part theologian, for everyone wants to know how things work and why they are made. When a child asks *how* the stars shine, he is asking a scientific question, and it is relatively easy to answer. When he asks *why* they shine, he is asking a theological question, and it is not easy to answer.

In response to these two questions of how and why, people develop theories and myths. A theory is simply a way of explaining things by relating cause to effect and ascertaining the various ways the elements of an event are related to each other. A myth is an analogy in the form of a story, metaphor, or simile that is used to make vivid an otherwise abstract theory. When modern man calls the world a great machine, he is using mythological language to illustrate his idea. When an electrician speaks about electric pulses and waves, he is using the mythological language of metaphor—electricity is compared to waves on the beach or the pulsation of blood in the bloodstream.

Scientists and theologians develop theories to explain the various ways they answer their respective questions, and often they use myths to lend veracity to their theories. For instance, original sin is not a brute fact of nature like stubbing one's toe on the corner of the dresser at midnight. It is a theory designed to explain the poignancy of man's plight, that man is somehow capable of the best but inevitably seems to choose the worst. Evolution is a theory designed to explain the variety in animal and vegetable life. When Charles Darwin took his famous trip on the Beagle, he had been vaguely discontented with the traditional ways of explaining things, and because of his observations on the similarities and dissimilarities of the flora and fauna he saw, he developed a theory about their relationships.

Now, a theory is neither true nor false, as some would like to claim. It either explains things well or it does not; it is either adequate or inadequate. One should sit very loosely on his convictions regarding theories because a better theory might come along— one which does a better job of explanation. A theory, then, is not a fact. It helps to explain the facts. It sets

28

them in relationship with each other so that a person can see the connections.

A theory is an attempt to answer a question, and the question is generally aroused by some puzzlement. The scientific question is aroused by the natural puzzlement over how things come to be the way they are and how they work. It is a question faced by cooks, mariners, schoolboys, and physicists. The theological question is always aroused by a puzzlement. It wonders why things are the way they are, and often more particularly, why man seems to be in such a perpetual mess.

Frequently, scientists make theological statements and then treat them like scientific theories. For instance, if someone claims that the evolution of the species involves progress and improvement, he has moved from science to theology. If a theologian talks about the origin of the world using the first three chapters of Genesis as data, he has passed from theology into science. In neither case should the person be taken very seriously.

One of the problems of modern society is its bias against theological questions. This secularity stems in part from the industrial and technological accomplishments of our civilization and has led to a situation in which the scientific pursuit has run wild. The pathos is that without theological considerations guiding him, man will likely end up like a headless monster, going nowhere but devouring everything in sight.

The Christian doctrine of Creation is about the merits of a scientific society's pursuits. The contest between the developers and the ecologists is religious, not scientific. Modern man knows how to preserve the natural beauty of the land and how to use it for economic development. Those questions are child's play for him. The real question is *why* he should preserve or develop the land. The question of "why" has been made all the more acute because of the vast success of the "how" questions in a modern industrial and technological society.

As a matter of fact, the "why" question has lagged so far behind the "how" question that man is now faced with such nonsensical accomplishments as "developed needs" and "stimulated markets." He has developed techniques before there is a need, and goods and gadgets before there is a market. Modern man is on a journey, but he is not sure why he is going and where he wants to go.

The stories in the first, second, and third chapters of Genesis are often called "creation accounts." Ironically, they are not creation accounts at all, for the biblical writers were not informed about how the world was made. They had some ideas about the matter, but they were largely taken over from other cultures and used for their own devices. For instance, the underlying theoretical structure of the first chapter was taken from the Babylonians, but the Hebrews used that account of the origin of the world to tell an entirely different story, the account of God's way with man. The biblical writers were concerned about the meaning of man.

It would be too strong to say that the biblical writers did not care about how the world was made, but it would be safe to say that it was not their prime concern. They were not driven by scientific questions. They were interested in the meaning of creation, not its mechanics.

When the Creed reads, "Maker of heaven and

earth", it is not describing how God made the world. It is referring to the issue of life's meaning. The author community which gave us the first chapter of Genesis had a hard time seeing much meaning in their lives. They were in a precarious position, existing at the whim and fancy of their adversaries. The things they held most dear had been destroyed when the Babylonians conquered them and sent them into exile. They had been an alien people in a strange land, and when they were allowed to return to their homeland, they found it desolate. They had ample reason to think life was chaos. The chapter speaks of how God brings order out of the chaos of nature, but it really is about the chaos of life. The ominous phraseology of the second verse refers to the dark ambiguity of people's lives. "The earth was without form and void and darkness was upon the face of the deep; and the Spirit of God was moving over the face of the waters" (Gen. 1:2). God, in their eyes, was moving amidst the formless void of their lives, and in the middle of this movement there comes the recurrent declaration that life is good.

The adequacy of the creation stories in the Old Testament does not depend on their coherence with modern scientific accounts of creation, for they were parabolic narratives about the meaning of life: Is there anything beyond and behind the visible chaos of life? Yes, God is moving to bring it to order and meaning, and the process reaches its peak in the coming of Jesus Christ.

Biblical man and modern man begin at the same point. They agree that man's situation is without form and void, but there they part company. Modern man has tried to coerce a meaning either by his accomplishments or his expectations, or else he has given up the quest. Biblical man was driven to faith. But modern man's desperate drive for success is a classic illustration of the false pride that overtakes a man when he tries to find meaning for his life through his own accomplishments. The racial pride that erupts in time of stress is an example of false pride in which a man clings to meaning through the illusion of his ethnic superiority. The rise of the drug culture among the middle classes is a sign of apathy in which people simply give up the accomplishments and the illusions.

The meaning of a man's life is hinged upon his sense of worth. He can think well of himself by what he has done, and by this he becomes his own creator. As with the idol maker of old, he finds meaning for his life by his skill and ability. Also, he can think well of himself because of his relationships. If he thinks of his relationships as accomplishments, then again he is his own creator because he has fashioned his idea of life's meaning by his ability to relate well to others. If he thinks of his relationships as the loving gifts of others, then his life will depend upon his faith in those who love him. He can also think well of himself by having faith in where he is going. His sense of worth is tied to his dreams and visions, and in this he is living in hope. Again, his dreams can be his own fabrications, and in this he becomes his own creator.

Living by accomplishments traps a person in the past. Older, retired people sometimes become bores because all they can do is talk about "the good old days" or recount their past accomplishments. Young people with little sense of the past are sometimes concerned only with building the future. Many times the supposed generation gap is really a conflict of past and future accomplishments. A past accomplishment by itself leads to a kind of apathy because it has no future, and apathy is often the malaise of the mature. They have fashioned their idea of life's meaning by what they have done, and gradually they see those accomplishments erode with the winds of change.

An apathy often found among middle-class women comes from having fashioned and created their idea of life's meaning by their relationships. They are known, almost exclusively, by their relationships to their husbands and children. They are Mrs. So-and-so and Johnny and Susy's mother. They want more. Husbands and children grow, but mother remains the same. An excessive dependence on the accomplishments of others results in apathy as the others gradually grow up and away.

The young with their visions and dreams eventually become apathetic when their dreams and visions are not fulfilled. Living on what they *will* do, they inevitably come up hard against what they have not done. No one's life is able to bear the burden of his dreams.

The ancient Hebrews writing the first chapter of Genesis could look back for encouragement to a great history including the patriarchs, Moses, King David, and the prophets, but their fear was that they had no future. Everything appeared uncertain. Their accomplishments were not enough. They were driven to a faith that the formlessness and void of life was being given order and purpose, not by the force of their accomplishments, but by the power of God moving amidst the chaos.

Man's sense of chaos has two sources. In the first place, the brute facts of life do not give him much comfort. In many ways life seems like a great dreadnought plowing through the seas unaware of man's small dingy being tossed by the waves of chance. There is so much hostility and indifference in life that it would seem almost unreal to think that it was going anywhere and had any meaning.

Also, once a man has tried and failed to fashion an image of life's meaning by his own skills, the chaos appears all the worse. This sense of having tried and failed is part of the poignancy of modern man. A good many young people pop pills, smoke pot, and drop acid because they have seen their parents' drive for meaning falter, and many of their parents have quietly given up also. Under the brutal pressure of events it does not take much for the false pride of achievement to give way to apathy.

The phrase "Maker of heaven and earth" refers to man's slide into apathy under the pressure of external events. It is speaking not so much about how the world was made as about God's control of life. Perhaps the black spiritual says it best: "He's Got the Whole World in His Hands." And if the world is in his hands, then the accomplishments of the past and the relationships of the present and a sense of the future are not man's actions but God's gift.

The way people treat their possessions indicates what they think of themselves. People acquire their possessions in one of three ways. They work for them, they receive them as gifts, or they steal them. If a man thinks well of himself and his work, he will treat his possessions with respect because he is caring for an extension of himself; homes kept by owners are generally better kept than those by tenants. If a man loves those who have given him his gifts, he will likely care for those gifts well as a gesture of affection. However, if he gains his possession by theft, he will likely abuse it. It has little value for him because it has not been earned or given. He has neither accomplished nor been loved. If a thing has been earned, then a person is made accountable by virtue of his work. If a thing is given, then a person is made accountable by virtue of his affection. If a thing is stolen, there is no accountability.

The phrase "Maker of heaven and earth" treats life as a gift, for man neither earned it nor stole it. But modern man actually treats life as a possession earned. He then is accountable to himself—which is one of the roots of his chaos, for he does not possess the wisdom and the power to control life as a possession earned.

In thinking of life as a thing earned, he actually engages in one of the most destructive forms of theft. If a wife responds to her husband's gift with the statement that she has earned it by giving him the best years of her life, she has made a gift into an earned possession. She robs herself of a gift of love and her husband of the joy of giving lovingly. She alienates her husband by thinking her husband's gift an achievement. Because of the dazzling success of his achievements, modern man treats the world as his possession and thereby robs himself of a gift. The result is chaos.

What happens to a person who has turned gifts into accomplishments? He is alienated. So too with the wife who achieves her gift—she loses her husband in the process of her achievements. The heart of life is in relationships, and accomplishments make sense only as expressions of relationships. If they stand alone, they are the source of false pride.

Modern man, by virtue of his astounding accomplishments, has come to think of his life as an achievement, and he has thus found himself alone and alienated in the chaos of his creation. He has developed nuclear energy—which has brought him up to the edge of the abyss—but, worse than that, he is left without a future. Since the world is in his hands, he has lost a sense of destiny, for history has not been kind to his attempts to coerce a meaning out of life through his accomplishments.

The choices are simple. Man can think his life an achievement, in which case he will inevitably find himself alone and alienated, either trying all the harder to achieve or simply giving up. He will be isolated in a false pride or alone in indifference. Life will be hard on his illusions. Or man can think of life as a gift given to be taken as a relationship of love, for the Maker of heaven and earth has created man to love him. In this case, man will see his accomplishments as an expression of that relationship, his life as an evidence of it, and his future as a continuation of it. In a society of accomplishment the Creed affirms that life is a gift and that amidst the chaos of man's creations God is working still to finish his creation.

5

Jesus Christ his only Son our Lord

The driver's license is a powerful symbol for the American male adolescent for by its acquisition a young man demonstrates his manhood. It is a time of high anticipation for the youth and deep foreboding for the parents. For the one it represents freedom and power, for the other, an anxiety about the safety of their son; the parents continue to be responsible for him, but they know they can no longer control him. Automobile insurance premiums skyrocket, scratches and dents mysteriously appear on the family car, arguments erupt over use of the car on Friday and Saturday nights, and television is watched nervously until the parents hear that familiar engine noise as the car rounds the corner at the end of the block.

The agony of parents whose boy is becoming a man might be rooted in a morbid compulsion to control the boy's life or in a concern for his welfare as he extends the circumference of his freedom. They are aware that freedom must come and they are aware of its hazards. They recall their own follies as well as newspaper accounts—like the article about the death of the high school football star who was killed while coming home from a late date because he fell asleep at the wheel. They know the propensity of young men to perform vehicular feats of derring-do, and they are acutely aware that they have given their son, in addition to his freedom, an awesome power with which he might even destroy himself.

Legally, their position is exquisitely delicate. Their scope of responsibility has been enlarged, for they are now accountable for their son's automotive actions as well as their own. However, their guilt has remained the same. If their son is at fault in a serious accident while driving the car, he would be guilty, not they; but the responsibility for the consequences of the accident, such as medical bills and therapy for the injured, would be placed squarely at their doorstep. While they were not the immediate cause of the accident, they established the conditions that made the accident possible. They gave their son the freedom and power with which to cause the accident. The boy would be guilty, but the parents would be responsible.

After an accident occurs, there are always some people who would blame the parents for allowing the son to drive. They would accuse the parents of giving him too much freedom and power. Indeed, the parents would probably blame themselves. But what were their choices? They could try to keep their son safely at home under wraps with the result that they might destroy the man within, or they could gradually give him freedom and power to become a man at his own risk.

When people say that God should stop all the pain and agony in the world, they are also saying that he should take away human freedom and power. The only way the parents of the boy could possibly save themselves and their son pain and grief would be to deny him his manhood. Human agony was not created by God. Its possibility was. The only way to take away man's pain and grief is to deprive him of his humanity, to deny him his freedom and power.

However, God has chosen not to deny man his humanity. He has chosen rather to participate in man's redemption. God chose to lead man by an act of sacrifice rather than by fiat. He could have eliminated the conditions of pain, namely freedom and power, by a tyrannical gesture of compulsive goodness, but such goodness, while having the guise of innocence, would have the substance of evil. Man would be destroyed in order to be saved.

One of the oldest elements in the Apostles' Creed is the ancient affirmation that Jesus Christ is Lord. People often think that his lordship is an expression of his deity. While there is some truth to that, it is not the whole truth, for the New Testament hinges Jesus' lordship on his sacrifice. Because he suffered and died he became Lord.

Parents face the same question of authority. Do a man and a woman become parents by an act of generation? Many would think so, but from the point of view of the child, the parents' real authority stems from their love for him. If there is no sacrificial love on the part of the parents for the child, the only authority the parents have is a coercive authority.

The New Testament is very clear in pointing out that the Creation is only part of Jesus' lordship. He is Lord not only because of the Creation, but also because of the Crucifixion and Resurrection. The parents' act of generation is without value and meaning if not fulfilled in the sacrifice of love. Begetting and giving birth do not make people parents. They merely establish the possibility of parenthood. To become a parent a person must care for and rear the child. Fathers and mothers are not abstract states of being. They are qualities of life.

In the prologue to his Gospel, John said that Jesus Christ was the agent of creation, but he goes on to point out that the act of creation was merely a prelude to the act of loving that which was made. Just as parents want children in order that they can extend the circumference of their love, so God in Jesus Christ made man in order to love him. Once man made a mess of his life, that act of love became a loving act of sacrifice.

Paul is explicit about the fact that Jesus' lordship is tied to his Crucifixion and Resurrection. In the Epistle to the Philippians Paul gave one of the most moving accounts anywhere of the consequences of the humiliation of Jesus Christ, concluding: "Therefore God has highly exalted him and bestowed on him the name which is above every name, that at the name of Jesus every knee should bow, in heaven and on earth and under the earth, and every tongue confess that Jesus Christ is Lord, to the glory of God the Father" (Phil. 2:9-11).

The lordship manifested in the Crucifixion was conclusively demonstrated in the Resurrection. Paul said that through the Resurrection Jesus Christ was designated Son of God and became man's Lord (Rom. 1:4). Jesus' authority came from what he did, and what he did was an extension and expression of who he was. His lordship is not an abstraction. It was established by his direct involvement and participation in human life. A mother's ability to influence her children does not rest in her abstract understanding of the nature

of motherhood. It comes from her having actually
loved them.

The Creed talks of belief "in Jesus Christ his only
Son our Lord." The phrase "Son of God" has been
one of the most troublesome in the history of the
church. For some it meant that Jesus Christ was somehow a lesser form of God than God the Father. In
fact, it means just the opposite. It witnesses to the belief that Jesus Christ is the enfleshment of God himself. The problem of its meaning goes back to biblical
genetics.

For the biblical man, the father placed his seed in
the womb of the woman and she acted something like
an incubator. The son was really an extension of the
father, and the mother only provided the environment. They knew about sperm, but not ova. Thus the
creedal phrase does not mean inferior to the father
but equal to him. The son is of the same stuff, for the
father passes his substance on to the son. Whether or
not one agrees with the biblical view of genetics is
not the issue. The question is what the biblical writers meant when they used the phrase "Son of God."
They meant that the son is of the same substance as
the father and, therefore, equal to him.

In other words, when God the Father sent his Son
into the world, he was sending himself. Jesus Christ
is not a divine surrogate or substitute, but the enfleshment of God himself. The Father, wishing to
save man from the debacle of his freedom and power,
redemptively involved himself in human life through
his Son, and this redemptive involvement, which cul-
minated in the Crucifixion and Resurrection, made
the Son man's Lord.

A belief in redemption through involvement is unattractive to many people because it is messy, time consuming, and inefficient. But that is what makes it unique. It is not a concern for the person's welfare that undergirds our concerns for cleanliness, order, and tidiness in home and society. Any mother with small children becomes acutely aware of the conflict between freedom for the children and order in the home, and she generally arrives at some haphazard, but functional, compromise. God in his providence keeps man away from the worst consequences of human freedom, but God's love still demands an apparent chaos. As a Father, God chose redemption over efficiency and utility.

The origin of a son's dilemma is in the decision of the parents to allow the son freedom and power. The origin of man's dilemma is in the decision of God to create him free with power to execute his freedom. In both cases the decisions were acts of love, for without them the son and man would be mere puppets, lacking the capacity to live freely. The speculative question about how God can allow so much misery ignores the substantial issue of man's freedom. Often those who speak so much about freedom are the ones who raise the question of why God does not stop the misery; they seem unaware of the inherent contradiction between their beliefs and wishes. Peace and order are only relative virtues in a free society; they are relative to justice. In a dictatorship they are absolute. Sinlessness is possible only for men without freedom and power.

Sin is essentially a negation, a denial. It is a corruption of goodness. It cannot stand by itself. It feeds off of goodness. Betrayal is a negation of trust. It exists only where there has first been trust and commitment.

Good and evil are not opposites existing equally and facing off in the battle of life. Evil is a corruption of goodness. Like a parasite it feeds off of goodness.

The irony of goodness is that it carries within itself the seeds of its own corruption, for goodness demands freedom. The boy misusing his freedom and power by speeding in his father's car was wrong, but he could not have been wrong until his father had trusted him with the freedom and power of the automobile. Someone cannot lie unless they first know the truth, and telling the truth becomes a virtue only when one has the possibility of telling a lie.

Paul Tillich observed that innocence is that state in which one does not have the possibility of being evil, and, therefore, is neither good nor evil. The possibility of evil has not yet arisen. A young girl before puberty cannot claim to have kept her virtue because, before puberty, she has not yet had the possibility of losing it. Once she passes puberty and begins to develop as a woman, then she has been given a freedom and power she did not have before. If she remains whole and intact, then she has a virtue. Before that time she was not virtuous, merely innocent.

Innocence is a prelude to humanity, for trust, love, and loyalty—all the virtues that make up the warmth and delight of life—require the possibility, but not the necessity, of their corruption. When referring to the story of the man and woman in the Garden of Eden, commentators sometimes say the man and woman were in a state of innocence. That is not quite true, for they were created with the possibility of evil. When God told them not to eat the fruit of the tree in the midst of the garden, he implied that they had a freedom and power of disobedience, else the command would have been pointless. Goodness is the experience of fidelity while living with the possibility of infidelity.

A person's response to the poignancy and irony of life is a reflection of his belief about God's relationship to him. Sometimes parents react to their children's misadventures by attempting to curtail the freedom and power. They deny the son the use of the car. They force a daughter to turn down dates and to stay at home. They try to spare themselves and their children grief and pain. Other parents accept what comes even if the boy ends up in the emergency ward of a hospital. They suffer with him but are willing to pay the price of his freedom; and, in spite of the risk, they offer him the use of the car after he is well. They are drawn into a closer relationship with him and with each other. The suffering becomes a source of communion much as the remembrance of Jesus' suffering becomes a source of communion in the Lord's Supper.

The pain and agony experienced by parents in the rearing of their children is one of the strongest bonds in family life, and the poignancy of the experience is intensified by the parents' realization that the expressions of their love in the gifts of freedom and power are the sources of the pain. Because of this the parents are willing to share their children's pain. They bear the consequences of the child's misuse of freedom and power.

Of course, the ultimate heartbreak is the child's rejection of the parent's loving involvement, but, ironically, the capacity to reject is also a gift. A relationship always carries within itself the seeds of its own destruction. Just as parents have the awesome power to abuse their children, so children have the awesome power to crucify their parents—precisely because their parents love them.

In *The Fall* Albert Camus said that if God had not become a man in the infant Jesus, there would not have been the slaughter of the innocents by Herod the Great.

> He was the source after all; he must have heard of a certain Slaughter of the Innocents. The children of Judea massacred while his parents were taking him to a safe place—why did they not die if not because of him? Those blood-spattered soldiers, those infants cut in two filled him with horror. But given the man he was, I am sure he could not forget them. And as for the sadness that can be felt in his every act, wasn't it the incurable melancholy of a man who heard night after night the voice of Rachel weeping for her children and refusing all comfort?

The conclusion is simple. God was responsible for that awesome tragedy because he established the conditions that made it possible. In creating the conditions in which evil might arise, God has implicated himself in the evil. And his response to this situation? He could not forget.

Jesus Christ is man's Lord because God could not forget. He was not someone sent by God to do his dirty business for him. He was God himself doing his own dirty work, and because God did his own dirty work, Jesus is Lord. He did not put an end to the chaotic and evil situation. He became a part of it—not to stop it but to redeem it.

6

Conceived by the Holy Spirit,
Born of the Virgin Mary

Bumper stickers are signs of the times. The modern American is strong on telling it like it is, but short on listening to what it's like. While the bumper sticker is a great way of telling someone else something, it shuts off the possibility of response. About the only thing a man can do is honk if he loves Jesus, but then he might be arrested for disturbing the peace.

Bumper stickers are a little short on dialogue, but they are the great American mobile bulletin board. Just as one might find the political persuasions, leisure-time proclivities, and economic interests of a citizen advertised on his bumper sticker, so one might find his theology.

A random sample would include such theological exhortations as "Give God a Chance," "Next Time Try Jesus," "Have Jesus, Will Share," "Smile, Jesus Loves You," plus several of the old favorites found in earlier times on fence posts and roadside signs like "Have You Found Jesus?", "Have You Made a Decision for Christ?", and "Have You Taken Jesus Into Your Heart?"

All of these have a common theme. They assume that man is looking for God and trying to find Jesus—as if God does not know where He is and Jesus is lost. Man goes looking for God in search of deep experiences, the final truth, or an absolute morality. In a somewhat blasphemous sense, bumper stickers assume that Jesus is just waiting around on some celestial street corner hoping for a pickup to make him Savior and Lord. As with all blasphemies, there is a contradiction involved. If someone *decides* to make Jesus Savior and Lord, Jesus is no longer Lord and, therefore, no longer Savior. Jesus is Lord, not because of man's decision but because of God's action. The person making the decision for Jesus would himself become lord because by his act of decision he would be making Jesus into something He previously was not.

This popular piety is, of course, merely a religious expression of a pervasive cultural ethos. It is widely held that it is up to man to make something of himself. A frustrated father customarily hurls hortatory warnings at his son along the lines that it is about time that the son get out and make something of himself—the obvious implication being that the son is not worth much at the present moment. If he works hard enough, he can remedy his dolorous situation through his own initiative.

In the relationship between God and man, one must always ask the question, Who initiates the relationship, God or man? Who chooses whom? Is Jesus lost so that the faithful must look around for him? Or is man lost, the Hound of Heaven pursuing him down the highways and byways of time? The question is so crucial that most people do not answer it consciously.

They make an assumption rather than a decision. In the kind of piety popular in America, the assumption has been that man is the initiator and God the responder.

The Christmas story is expressed creedally in the statement, "Conceived by the Holy Spirit, Born of the Virgin Mary." This belief is a conundrum to the man who thinks he is master of his own destiny and captain of his own fate. But it simply means that God took the initiative by enfleshing himself so that he might encounter man in terms man could understand. In other words, God put himself on the block of human existence.

The nature of Jesus Christ has always been a problem for the church. As with all institutions, the church's conflict has been polarized around two mutually contradictory points of view, with temporizers in the middle trying to please everyone while actually pleasing very few. On the one hand, there have been some who believed that Jesus Christ was essentially a realization of man's natural movement toward God; he became true man by reaching divinity through his goodness. On the other hand, there have been those who believed that Jesus Christ was the culmination of God's movement toward man. Rather than seeing man as moving toward God, they believed that man was fleeing from him. Adam and Eve hid from God in the Garden of Eden after their fall. They were not out looking for him; he was looking for them.

The first group would see Jesus as the true man attaining deity; the second would see him as the true God becoming man. Those who held the middle ground between these two poles of thought tried to reconcile what they thought was the best of both positions, with the result that in their minds God moved slightly toward man and man inched a little toward God. Jesus Christ in their eyes became a *tertium quid*, a kind of third party who was neither man nor God—a superman and a demigod.

For instance, many Christians who say they believe that God became a man in Jesus Christ have a hard time believing that he really became fully a man with all the limitations of human frailty. Some of them even speak as if the infant in the cradle were self-consciously aware that he was the Savior of the world. Other Christians have a hard time with the deity of Christ and are prone to see in Jesus the highest of human achievements. They think of him as a spiritually sensitive man who morally made it to the top.

The statement in the Apostles' Creed concerning Jesus' conception by the Holy Spirit and birth of the Virgin Mary is an example of a profound symbol. Part of the irony of the church is that the debate has usually revolved around the symbols rather than the issues. As with a great many arguments in the church, such as the credibility of Genesis and the edibility of Jonah, the debate about the virginity of Mary misses the point. The authenticity and thus the deity of Jesus Christ are not guaranteed by Mary's virginity, but by the conception by the Holy Spirit. The point is that the birth of Jesus Christ took place at the initiative of God. The virginity of Mary merely points to the passivity of man and thus to Jesus' humanity.

Man's freedom consists not so much in his choice of God as in the quality of his response to the fact that God has chosen him. Freedom is not a random choice executed in a vacuum. It is a response to an initiative.

One has the freedom to determine the quality of his response to those realities thrust on him beginning with his birth. Some people are apparently dragged kicking and screaming into life, others creep in and out of life with a dull resignation, and still others, in spite of all hazards and perils, seem to dance through life. Their freedom is not in their birth; it is in the way they respond to life after their birth, namely, in the quality of their lives.

The Apostles' Creed, in saying that the movement is from God to man, also says that man either cannot or will not move toward God on his own initiative. It also says that life is inherently good, for God could not have become a man if man were inherently evil. Is man's problem that he does not know enough and needs a moral teacher to show him the way out of his dilemma? A new Moses to lead him out of his peril? If one assesses man's plight in terms of moral and psychic ignorance, then Jesus Christ is only a teacher of goodness, a giver of moral precepts. The movement then is from man to God, for man has within himself the ability to straighten out his life if he can learn how.

If man's problem is that he is inherently perverse, that he is a sophisticated beast of prey not too recently removed from the jungle, then he is essentially unredeemable. About all that can be done is to apply occasional palliatives designed only to ameliorate his sickness but not cure it. Economically, this appears in Karl Marx's definition of the necessity of class warfare. Psychologically, it is found in Freud's neverending war of the worlds within.

The modern world is often the victim of either a facile optimism about man's opportunities for goodness or an enervating pessimism that numbers its wars I, II, and possibly III. The competitive mentality of modern capitalism operates under the same assumption of necessary conflict as does communism, capitalism seeing the conflict among its own while communism sees it as being with outsiders.

In a mind-set which sees man as gradually improving morally, Jesus Christ serves as a type of moral hero. When the outlook assumes conflict, there is hardly a place for a savior at all unless it be at the end, as an escape hatch from a hopeless situation; man has to be written off before he can be redeemed. In both cases the belief that God is moving toward man to redeem him is either beside the point or a charming impossibility. It is small wonder that modern man has a hard time with the Christian faith, for it does not confirm his generally held beliefs; it questions and contradicts them.

A father knows the miserable things he does to his children, but he seems to know this only on reflection after the fact. A man may go from job to job repeating the same personal mistakes that cost him his job each time, with some glimmer in the back of his mind of the origins of his difficulty. Some women go from marriage to marriage terminating them each because of some self-destructive propensity for marrying the same type of unstable man.

The Christian faith has none of the easy optimism of moral-improvement-through-education or the deadly pessimism of jungle warfare. The belief that Jesus Christ was born of the Virgin Mary places God squarely in humanity, for it is a statement of the humanity and vulnerability of God. He has put himself on the block of human existence. The conception by the Holy Spirit puts to rest the sanguine notion that man is on a gradual moral escalator, for the birth of Jesus Christ took place at the initiative of God.

The belief that God became a man in Jesus Christ, in addition to saying something about God, says something about man. It is an obvious statement about the extent of God's love for man, but it is also a more subtle statement about the nature of man's malaise. Man's problem is profound and deep, else God would not have had to become a man. It is not hopeless, else God could not have become a man.

The things that get a person in trouble are generally not his obvious vices, but his virtues. It is good that a boy should become a man and exhibit his manhood. It is good that, when a girl reaches a certain age, she should become a woman and act out her womanhood. But the boy's virtue of manliness may lead him to a tragic accident, and the girl's virtue of womanliness may lead her to tragedy as well. The risk is well worth taking, however, for the sources of evil are also the well-springs of virtue. The good is turned to evil only when it is used to prove what one should be able to assume, namely, that manhood and womanhood are good.

The source of the evil is the insecurity that prompts a boy to *prove* he is a man, or a girl to *prove* she is a woman. Adam and Eve wanted to be like God and know everything—that is, they wanted security and certainty. They wanted to make it on their own and, as with the boy and girl, they were then compelled to prove themselves. The irony is that their attempts to prove themselves made their plight all the worse, for they shut themselves off from God.

It does not take much wit to see that man is in a

precarious situation and spends much of his time seeking security. This he does by using such virtues as his intelligence, strength, ability, and even morality. So his virtues become his vices because in his insecurity he uses them to his own destruction. A woman tries to guarantee her husband's love and thereby destroys it. A young girl tries to buy a boy's esteem by being free with her affections and reaps his contempt instead. A man tries to prove his strength and ends up demonstrating his weakness.

In the eleventh century an Englishman named Anselm wrote a book called *Cur Deus homo?* [Why God man?] It is a question that has disturbed countless believers before Anselm and since. The question stands at the heart of the Christian faith, and the only answer that makes much sense is that God is responsible for man's malaise. God made the conditions and possibilities for the mess man is in. God is responsible. But it is a loving responsibility. There was really no possibility of ignoring the malaise or removing it by fiat. God put himself on the block of human existence to bring about the redemption of man through a direct and immediate participation in man's life. He had to stand where man stands, else he could not speak to man, much less redeem him. In the words of the author of the Epistle to the Hebrews, he became the "pioneer and perfector of our faith" (Heb. 12:2).

God became a man—that is, Jesus Christ was conceived by the Holy Spirit and born of the Virgin Mary— because God was responsible for man's malaise. God gave man the freedom and power, and man brought about his ruin with the very gifts of freedom and power.

The deity and humanity of Jesus Christ is the heart

of the issue. His deity is essential because man no longer needs surrogates and substitutes for God; he has had enough of them. The conception by the Holy Spirit points to the belief in the authenticity of God's presence in Jesus Christ. Man is not getting some second-hand information or indirect relationship. Jesus Christ is God himself meeting man in terms man can understand.

The humanity of Jesus Christ is just as important, for not only does it say that man was good enough for God to assume his flesh, but also that God chose to relate to man in terms of human experience. One of the disabling qualities of so much of religion has been its ethereal and unworldly qualities. It seems to have no connection with human experience. Indeed, it is often used as a means of escaping life rather than redeeming it.

Man, for better or for worse, is married to his five senses. This is the way he knows, and if God is to reveal and relate himself to man, then it has to be in the flesh. Man is physical, and the revelation and relationship cannot live without that physical reality. God's revelation and redemption were not limited by God, but by man. He had to speak man's language by living man's experience, and the only way to do that was to become a man.

Some people have said that Jesus Christ is not fully human for some rather good but misplaced reasons. They want to protect God, to circumscribe him from the terrors and tumults of time. They believe that God did not fully become a man. He just appeared in human form without the full consequences of human life. He did not enter man's loneliness, his anxieties, his frustrations, his joys, and his rewards. Jesus Christ just floated through life without really touching it or being touched by it. As with most efforts to protect, this one too is without authenticity. God is not so fragile that he cannot endure death and destruction.

The enfleshment of God in Jesus Christ is first of all an affirmation of the fundamental goodness of man. The incarnation of God is a reaffirmation of the Creation. If the Creation is fundamentally good, then Jesus Christ is possible. The enfleshment of God is not something alien. It is the consequence of a good creation gone askew because of man's abuse of freedom and power.

The conviction that Jesus Christ is the enfleshment of God rests in the conviction that man's problem is beyond his ability to correct. It goes to the roots of his character. Man does not need to *know* more, that is, his problem is not ethical. A new and better moral code will not help him. His problem is in the heart of his being. He has misused and abused the gifts of freedom and power by using them to gain independence from the giver.

It was the custom in the villages of England that when a man of the village died, the bell in the church would be tolled to signal his death to the community. When this occurred, it was natural that people would wonder for whom the bell tolled. John Donne wrote his famous lines (*Devotions* 17) in this context:

No man is an island, entire of itself; every man is a piece of the continent, a part of the main; if a clod be washed away by the sea, Europe is the less, as well as if a promontory were, as well as if a manor of thy friends or of thine own were; any man's death diminishes me, because I am involved in mankind, and therefore never send to know for whom the bell tolls, it tolls for thee.

God is not an island entire of himself. He is involved in mankind. When the bell tolled man's misery and death, God was diminished. He had given man the possibilities of his death and misery. The bell tolled for God, and in the fulness of time God sent himself by sending his Son. The incarnation of God in Jesus Christ is the inevitable consequence of God's creation. Jesus Christ is an affirmation of the goodness of creation and a recognition of its misery.

7

Suffered under Pontius Pilate,
Was crucified, dead, and buried:
He descended into hell

The doctrines of hell and damnation are seldom self-applied by those ardently believing them. Believers in creation and salvation customarily think of themselves as created by God and saved by Jesus Christ, and believers in hell and damnation almost always apply these concepts to someone else. Occasionally, one might run across some benighted soul who lives with the constant dread of eternal damnation, but he is generally referred to a psychiatrist on the assumption that he is a victim of emotional illness rather than an example of theological sophistication. Hell is an "other guy" belief, and such comfort as it might have for believers is largely negative—one is thankful one has managed to escape it, or one is pleased that someone else is "really going to get theirs."

A belief designed for the "other guy" is generally without merit, for it in no way illuminates one's own life. It is self-righteous and vindictive, qualities hardly commended in the Christian lexicon of virtues. In addition to those lamentable liabilities, the hell and damnation doctrine has encouraged the lurid imaginings of the lunatic fringe of the faith.

Part of the problem is that damnation has been thought of as an act of God, and hell his creation. Damnation was something God did to someone he did not like, and hell was the place where that something was done. Ironically, man has attributed to God what man did himself, for human freedom and power contain within themselves the ultimate abuse, the rejection of God's graciousness. Damnation is something a man does to himself when he cuts himself off from God, and hell is that condition, rather than place, in which a man decides to live alone by his own wits. Hell occurs when a man becomes captain of his fate and master of his soul.

Hell and damnation are the consequences of what man does to himself with his God-given gifts. They are the awful consequences of freedom, for in making man good, God made him with the capacity to destroy himself. Man had to have the freedom finally and conclusively to reject God, else his freedom would have been a charade.

In the middle of the Apostles' Creed three successive phrases come like hammer blows: "suffered under Pontius Pilate, was crucified, dead, and buried, he descended into hell." Some believers bothered by the idea of hell sometimes eliminate the last of the phrases. They prefer to believe that hell has no place in a Christian statement of faith. However, hell is the inevitable consequence of the rejection of God implied in the suffering and Crucifixion of Jesus Christ. In that event the righteousness of man crucified the graciousness of God. Hell had to follow.

Some are bothered by the doctrines of hell and damnation because they ask how a good God could condemn men and send them to hell as a punishment. They do not think it fair or just, and they believe that if God were really a loving God that he would never send anyone to hell. They, of course, ask the wrong question. The appropriate question is, Does God allow a man to send *himself* to hell by rejecting God's graciousness?

Central to the Christian faith is the idea of freedom, that man is responsible for his life before God. If one believes in freedom, he is compelled to believe in the possibility but not the necessity of hell and damnation. Freedom implies the possibility of rejection, failure, and destruction, and any attempt to do away with freedom in the belief that hell and damnation are not nice ideas will reduce man to robot status. His salvation will be purchased with the price of his destruction.

Hell and damnation are the implications of freedom, for the Crucifixion of Jesus Christ is man's rejection of God. Rather than God consigning men to hell, men dragged God through their own hell by their Crucifixion of Jesus Christ. It was man who sent God to hell, for if God loved man, He would be compelled to endure man's rejection. Freedom is not a charade, for God has paid the full measure for man's freedom.

The hammer-like quality of these phrases in the middle of the Creed indicates their significance. The suffering of Jesus Christ is very carefully located in time. It is not some kind of suffering-in-general. It is a suffering under a particular political ruler known to historical documents outside the Christian tradition. The Christian faith finds itself rooted in history and is thus divorced from obtuse spiritual speculation. Its pivotal point was an actual event of degradation.

Frequently, the suffering and Crucifixion of Jesus Christ raises a profound question among men. They want to know why it was necessary for Jesus to suffer. "Why couldn't God just wipe out man's misery and sin and make him sinless?" they often ask. It is, of course, akin to the question of why God permits the sin and misery in the first place. Why doesn't God allow men to say "no," or having allowed it, why does he let them suffer the consequences when they say it?

One of the disturbing things about the gospel is the revelation that God takes man more seriously than man takes himself. A loving God will simultaneously demand excellence from his creatures and exhibit mercy when the creature fails. The same God who judges man is also the God who redeems him. Justice is the expectation of the best, and the ultimate insult God could heap upon man would be to expect less than the best. A parent who does not expect excellence from his children is one who does not care about being a parent or has written off the children. The parental shrug of, "What else would you expect of Susy?" expresses a contempt for Susy. The expectation of less than the best is a way of writing people off, of saying, "Don't inconvenience me with your failures."

For God to write off man's malaise as if to say that one really could not expect much else from man would not be merciful. It would be cruel contempt. If God were to hold man in contempt, he would have to hold himself in contempt, for he made man. The wistful hope that God might just wipe out malaise without pain is an example of man's contempt for himself.

A grievous insult, a deep psychic wound, a willful rejection—these cannot be passed over lightly by people who take themselves and others seriously. Something has to be done to take away the insult, heal the wound, and reconcile the rejected. Until a man takes himself seriously, he can never take himself joyfully.

In taking man seriously, God allowed himself to be dragged into the pit of man's destruction. Man's defiant misuse and abuse of his freedom and power led inevitably, because God is a loving God, to the suffering under Pilate and the descent into hell. There was no other way if God were not to reject himself by rejecting his creation. The love of God is not an easy doctrine designed to comfort cruel men with easy speeches. It is a tough doctrine spelling out the consequences of man's abuse of his gifts.

The words "crucified, dead, and buried" leave no doubt about the central issue. One word would have done it, but three were used so that even the slowest or most perverse among us would get the point. God suffered the consequences of man's freedom. In Jesus Christ he experienced death. This is an awesome belief, for it goes beyond the reaches of the imagination.

One might wonder how a person can experience death without dying, but on reflection each man experiences many deaths. Death is the experience of severed relationships. Death causes anxiety about death. Long meaningful associations are concluded irrevocably. Little deaths afflict all men. A family fight that sends a son out in anger against a father is a death for more than the son and the father. The mother stands aside and yet participates in the death because she loves them both. Perhaps the most common form of death in a mobile society is moving away from friends. Things are never the same, and indeed sometimes the closest of friends are lost. When a husband dies after a long and happy marriage, it is not uncommon to hear the widow say, "Something in me died when Jack went." The experience of death is a stranger to no one, and if God would speak to man in terms man could understand, he had to live through the experience of death. God assumed man's lot and experienced his death.

If God could not speak to man in his grief, loneliness, and pain, he could not speak to man at all, for it is at these points that man's answers fade while his questions remain. The theoretical and speculative questions about why the misfortunes happen are never answered. God did not respond to agony with an argument. He responded with himself. He assumed man's plight and bore it. He reached out across the gulf of time, space, and deity to live and die as a man.

The suffering under Pontius Pilate, the Crucifixion, death, and burial, the descent into hell point to God's assessment of man's misery and grandeur. On the one hand, man's plight was so pervasive and extensive that nothing else would do but that man be taken that seriously by God, and on the other hand, his potentialities and possibilities are so grand that the sacrifice was not misspent. Too often the cross is used to point exclusively to the misery of man without an awareness that it also assumes his natural grandeur; unless man is valuable, the suffering, death, and descent are wasted.

One of the most useful images in the New Testament about man's plight is that of alienation or estrangement. Reading Paul's letters on the theme of estrangement and reconciliation, one has the feeling that Paul is curiously modern, for alienation is one of the dominant themes in contemporary thought. Paul's point is clear: Man is alienated from others and even from himself because of his alienation from God.

The themes of alienation and estrangement speak very clearly to the isolation and loneliness of a modern, industrial society. But one of the problems facing the lonely man is the means of reconciliation. Modern thought has been very long on delineating the misery of man, but very short on pointing out the graciousness of God. Original sin, which is that doctrine that speaks of the inevitability of human malaise, is probably the only doctrine in the Christian lexicon of belief that can be amply illustrated by the morning newspaper. Depth psychology has put flesh on the dry bones of original sin, spelling out the dynamics of man's propensity to destroy himself under the illusion that he is saving himself.

The modern industrial state is not congenial to the welfare of man. His feet and legs were not designed to walk on concrete. His lungs were not made to inhale smog. The impersonality of the giant corporations was not developed to help a gregarious animal like man to live comfortably. Computers, identification numbers, lines of authority are all alien to man's fundamental state; they make man a stranger in his own land. The works of his mind and hands ironically have left him an alien.

The alienation and estrangement of which Paul spoke were primarily racial, religious, and ethnic, and those lines of hostility are as virulent today as they were in his day. To a degree, his contemporaries felt the alienation of the state in the form of the Roman Empire; but, whatever the origins of the estrangement, apparently both Paul and modern man have had the same experience. Wanting to feel at home in the world and at ease within, they feel strangers without and torn apart within.

When theology says that men have been reconciled in Jesus Christ, the question is immediately raised about the nature of estrangement. Is man's hostility rooted in his ignorance, and thus cured by education? Is it rooted in his anthropoidal past, and thus a hopeless residue of bestiality? Is it rooted in his alienation from God? A belief that God became a man, suffered, and died to reconcile man to himself also says that man's hostility arises from his alienation from God. Any talk about peace is a mere placebo unless there is peace with God.

One of the richest Pauline images is that of justification by grace through faith, for in it Paul speaks of the constant predicament of a sense of condemnation. One of the principal means by which societies and governments control their members and citizens is the device of inducing a sense of having been condemned, a feeling of unease and insecurity. The society then claims to accept the distressed and give them a feeling of security and acceptance if they fulfill certain obligations. It can be the willingness to die for one's country, the payment of exorbitant initiation fees and monthly dues in a country club, a willingness to accept social debasement, and even a confession of sins.

Of course, the feeling of having been condemned does not originate with the societies. They merely use it for their own benefit. The feeling comes from the universal sense of failure and inadequacy. The world is a threat, and no man ever completely masters it. He lives with an inner fear of his own unworthiness that can never be removed or reduced by the palliatives of organizations and the placebos of human schemes.

The Christian faith takes seriously man's sense of having been condemned. It does not diminish man by saying that his deepest feelings are illusions and falsehoods. By saying that man is justified by grace through faith, Christianity is also saying that man's sense of having been condemned is real and not an illusion. He *has* failed, and his sense of failure is not just a misfortune but possibly a new beginning.

The coming of Jesus Christ, his suffering, death, and descent into hell all point to a radical estimate of the depth of man's malaise. His guilt cannot be dismissed as a mere feeling which he can be talked out of. His estrangement is so deep that he is trapped in it, and every measure he takes to get himself out will only strengthen the bonds of alienation. In other words, man is in bondage, and every gesture towards freedom is merely one more turn of the screw on his fetters.

The insecurity and frailty of man's life move him to find stability, meaning, and purpose. It is the attempt to find that security that is the source of his malaise and misery. The things that he uses to save himself enslave him.

The pursuit of social acceptance, economic security and emotional stability all have the same result. The things designed to free a man trap him. The counterculture of the protesters is every bit as much a trap as the mediocrity of the establishment. In biblical language man uses an idol to gain his security, and the idol of his fashioning becomes his own master; he is hoisted by his own petard.

In the New Testament man is thought to be in bondage to the forces of evil finally personified in the figure of Satan. In our day, Satan has fallen on hard times; he has largely been laughed out of serious discussion. It has been suggested more than once that perhaps the chief victory of Satan in the twentieth century is his ability to persuade modern man that he does not exist. If an adversary can persuade his foe that he does not exist, then the battle is all but won. No one guards himself against a nonexistent enemy.

The doctrine of the devil is built upon the conspiratorial theory of evil. Modern man has by and large adopted the piecemeal theory of evil in which all the sin and misery are chances and incidents in the affairs of men; they occur because a man has made a mistake either through ignorance or hostility. The doctrine of the devil, on the contrary, in addition to seeing human evil as a product of individual or communal failures, looks at it as a part of a vast conspiratorial network in which a Power is using man's failures in a pattern of destruction.

However, looking at the evidence of human corruption and degradation, one has to decide whether or not the vast sum of human misery is a product of incidental chances or a result of a vast conspiracy against mankind. After the revelations of the Cosa Nostra it is easy to believe the conspiratorial theory of evil. The black man is certainly familiar with the conspiracy of white men to deprive him of his rights. Some moderns are prone to label the doctrine of the devil as mythology, and while some of the graphic images that have grown up around the doctrine are relics of the past, the main idea is uncomfortably contemporary.

A belief in the conspiracy of evil is not a form of paranoia. It means that evil is not happenstance and chance accident. The devil does not make people do stupid and evil things. The doctrine means that behind the temptation is a tempter. While man is responsible for his life, he is contending with more than himself. He is contending with a pattern, a system, a power of destruction.

The idols he makes to give him security in his insecurity become his demons. He may fashion his own hell from the good things given him by God, but his descent into his hell is finally accomplished through the demonic force of his idols. The irony is that man becomes the victim of his own creations, with the result that what he has made becomes his master.

The world as a system of evil, the devil as a conspirator of destruction, hell as a state in which men get exactly what they want, demons as idols which have come back to haunt their creators—all are symbols of what man has done with the goodness of God. In his insecurity and loneliness, man has tried to justify himself and make something of his life by his accomplishments. All of this crucified Jesus Christ, and it is this hell into which he descended. God submitted himself to the whole conspiracy, the demonic system.

Roman law and Jewish religion, some of the finest products of human goodness, were the twin forces that conspired to put to death the graciousness of God.

God's mercy was not crucified by the obviously evil men, but by the obviously good men, who used their goodness to create the hell of the Crucifixion.

God became a man and endured the hell man had made because He was responsible for the malaise, having given man the conditions under which he could fashion that hell. God became a man so that he might speak to man out of the conditions in which man lives, so that he could break the power of the demonic system of evil and give man his freedom. He suffered as a man suffers, experienced the loneliness and rejection, died, and descended into man's hell.

This is faith's radical assessment of man's existence. It is radical in its assessment of the scope and depth of man's malaise, and radical in its response to the malaise. The Creed asserts that God sends no one to hell. Instead he goes to hell himself because he is responsible for the conditions that made hell possible. And before his creation could be redeemed, the power of that conspiracy of evil, that system of destruction, had to be broken. On the cross God endured and withstood the onslaught of human goodness, and prevailed.

8

He rose again from the dead;
He ascended into heaven

On Good Friday, during the traditional services from high noon to three o'clock, seven meditations are customarily developed around the seven last words of Jesus Christ on the cross. In one of them, the cry of dereliction, "My God, my God, why hast thou forsaken me?" is usually treated as a cry of abandonment pointing to the agony of Christ as he endured the Crucifixion. This is a pity, for its meaning is just the opposite. It is a cry of assurance, a prayer of confidence amidst dereliction and despair.

One of the remarkable things about the accounts of the Crucifixion in the Gospels is their sparseness. There is no maudlin sentimentality, no prying into Jesus' psychological and emotional state—just a bare recital of the events and circumstances of his death. The supposed cry of dereliction, far from being a clue to his emotional state, is a declaration of faith amidst a chorus of disbelief.

The supposed cry of dereliction is actually a quotation from Psalm 22:1. With the aim of saving writing material, it was a literary habit of the time to quote only the first line of a passage of Scripture to indicate the use of the whole passage. In his reference to the cry Matthew intended to show that Jesus, while enduring the pain and agony of the cross, recited familiar passages of Scripture to give himself aid and comfort.

The Psalm's first line may sound like a cry of dereliction, but the whole of the Psalm is an affirmation of faith in God's deliverance in the middle of desolation. It is also an uncanny description of the details of the Crucifixon.

> Yea, dogs are round about me;
> a company of evildoers encircle me;
> they have pierced my hands and feet—
> I can count all my bones—
> they stare and gloat over me;
> they divide my garments among them,
> and for my raiment they cast lots.
> (Ps. 22:16–80).

In addition to being a cry of anguish the Psalm is also a song of praise. It expresses the loneliness and agony of a man undergoing pain and persecution and, along with that, his hope in God's abiding presence.

> For he has not despised or abhorred
> the affliction of the afflicted;
> and he has not hid his face from him,
> but has heard, when he cried to him.
> (Ps. 22:24).

That is not a cry of dereliction. It is a song of assurance. The oppressed and persecuted shall eventually "proclaim his deliverance to a people yet unborn, that he has wrought it" (Ps. 22:31).

Matthew was setting the stage for the Resurrection of Jesus Christ so that the Resurrection would not be discontinuous with the Crucifixion. In the midst of his agony and death, Jesus Christ did not break unity with God the Father, and that unity with God the Father was the issue in the Crucifixion and the Resurrection.

Christian theologians often treat the Resurrection in one of two ways. Some say it was all in the minds of the disciples; by the power of their faith they encountered Jesus after his death. Others say the Resurrection was a physical resuscitation of Jesus' dead flesh. In both views the Resurrection is discontinuous with the Crucifixion. It appears as if nothing was carried over from the Crucifixion to the Resurrection or was present in the Crucifixion as well as the Resurrection.

If it were merely in the minds of the disciples, then there was obviously no continuity between Jesus of Nazareth and the risen Christ. Jesus of Nazareth existed independently of their perception of him, but the risen Christ was the creation of their perception in faith. If Jesus' Resurrection was a resuscitation of his flesh, one might well wonder if anything endured and abided. Did he become extinct and then come into existence again?

The common, garden variety doctrine would probably hold that the original belief of the church was resuscitation, and that modern sophisticates and liberals have substituted in its place the Jesus-of-the-faithful-imagination theory. But the fact is that both are deviations from the earliest understanding of the Resurrection in the New Testament, that of Paul in the fifteenth chapter of 1 Corinthians. In Paul's thought the Resurrection was not a resuscitation; it was a transformation. It was not a creation of faith; faith was created by the Resurrection experiences.

The Resurrection of Jesus Christ was clearly disbelieved by, doubted by, and confounding to the disciples, and with that confusion—coupled with their general slowness of heart during his earthly ministry—it is very hard to see how their strength of faith could have been the origin of the Resurrection. Jesus was not forced out of death by the power of their faith. They were forced out of doubt by the power of his Ressurrection.

In addition, Paul points out that "flesh and blood cannot inherit the kingdom of God" (1 Cor. 15:50), which means that the Resurrection was not a resuscitation of dead flesh. Indeed, a moment's reflection shows that life is not merely the adequate functioning of the body's vital organs. When a person has been lingering near death for some time, one often hears someone say, "It'll be a blessing when he goes. He really hasn't been alive for the last few months."

When one begins to think about the Resurrection, one is forced to define two key words: life and death. Since most people assume answers about life and death without ever thinking them through, they run into trouble with the Resurrection. Life is customarily associated with the functioning of the body's vital organs, and death with their cessation. The heart stops working, the brain is destroyed, the life systems of the body collapse—these are all aspects of death, and they all have to do with the flesh.

But life is something more than the operation of the physical system. The Bible is full of images about life. Paul said that, for him, living was Christ (Phil. 1:21), which means that his life was a living relationship with Jesus Christ. In his great high priestly prayer

Jesus prays: "And this is eternal life, that they know thee the only true God, and Jesus Christ whom thou hast sent" (John 17:3). For both Paul and John life was not so much a physical functioning as it was a vital relationship with God.

The fear of death in most men is not the fear of the end of physical existence, though sometimes it includes fear of the pain involved in a terminal illness. The fear, rather, is that the end of physical existence means the termination of relationships. Parents worry that if they die there will be no one to care for their children. A man and wife who have spent years of life together have a hard time thinking of life apart from that relationship. The ensuing loneliness appears as a curse.

The end of the physical functions is feared because it means that life itself, the highly prized relationships, will end. The bereaved will be left with only memories. Life is largely relationships and, ultimately, relationship with God. Death is the termination of those relationships. This realization is what makes people weep at the death of a loved one. It is what causes a poignant sadness in the mind of a man as he faces his own death.

Part of the problem with the Bible in this matter is that people almost invariably equate the word "body" with "flesh," while in Paul the two were clearly distinguished. In the fifteenth chapter of 1 Corinthians Paul claims that the body of flesh, that is to say, physical functioning, is changed at the resurrection into a body of spirit. Apparently, he uses the word "body" with much the same meaning as we today use "person" or "personality."

In Paul's thought the resurrection is a transformation of the personality of flesh into a personality of spirit. The word "flesh" for him means perishability, weakness, dishonor, dust. The word "spirit" means imperishability, strength, honor, heaven. In these terms, the resurrection is not a resuscitation of the flesh but a transformation of a person from weakness, dishonor, and death, to a person of strength, honor, and life.

The word "spirit" means unseen power, with the emphasis on the power. Its root meaning is wind. While the wind may not be seen in itself, its effects are clearly visible. The belief in the resurrection as a transformation of a body of weakness to a body of strength does not necessarily mean that the so-called "spiritual body" is invisible. The emphasis is on power.

The body of weakness, or the personality of death, is that system of life in which a man tries to fashion his security and meaning through his own virtues and goodness. He develops a way of life that makes him feel worthwhile. Of course, his virtues are corrupted in the process and become what Saint Augustine called "splendid vices." His virtues and powers end up becoming his demons, for he must constantly serve them to keep meaning in his life and to maintain his security. If they collapse, he dies. He ends up a spiritual and moral cripple who spends his life propping himself up, all the while becoming more entangled in his sticks and crutches.

There has been a strong tradition that man can survive death because of an immortal and everlasting substance in him called his soul. At man's physical cessation the soul is said to be freed from the flesh. Sometimes this view is confused with the biblical view, but it is in fact quite alien to it, for the Bible does not think in terms of the immortality of anyone except God. Rather than the immortality of the soul, the biblical belief is in the resurrection of the body.

What was there about Jesus Christ which enabled him to survive the experience of death? Some would say that he had to survive since he was the enfleshment of God. That point of view would, of course, make his life and suffering a charade. There had to be the risk that God would die, that in the very being of God, the Son and Father would be alienated to the point of destruction. If that were not a possibility, then the Crucifixion and Resurrection were mere mechanical symbols.

The supposed cry of dereliction from the cross provides us with an understanding of the Resurrection. The experience of psychic nakedness, a sense of vulnerability, is the source of man's attempt to live by his idols, his demonic goodness. Out of his insecurity he tries to fashion security by his own strength. Man's psychic peril leads him to the pragmatic atheism of living as though God were not. At the time of his gravest peril on the cross, Jesus in agony cried out his trust. Under the onslaught of man's demonic goodness and the experience of abandonment, he did not break his unity with God the Father. Jesus made it through man's perils.

In the temptations of Jesus at the beginning of his ministry he was tantalized by the devil to use his own strength and goodness as a means of insuring his safety and survival. He refused each time, not claiming to be good, but relying rather on his Father's relationship with him. The systems of virtue and goodness by which men try to save themselves were not the source of his power. It was, rather, his trust. As a matter of fact, it was human goodness that was crucifying him. He broke the barriers of death because he trusted in his Father rather than in his own power and virtue.

The death of Jesus Christ on the cross spelled out the possibility that the internal relationship within God might be destroyed, and, therefore, God would be destroyed. Thus, the Resurrection of Jesus Christ is God's conquest of sin and death, that is, God's conquest of man's attempt to live by his achieved goodness, resulting in alienation from God.

The Resurrection of Jesus Christ in the Gospels often raises the question of his appearance. People ask whether, had there been cameras at the time, his body could have been photographed. This type of speculation misses the point. It is clear that if the Resurrection were the transformation of a person from a body of weakness to a body of strength, there would be a continuity between the two. Whether the new body could be photographed no one can say. The important thing to recognize is that the disciples were able to see him, and not because of the strength of their faith.

One of the remarkable things about the resurrection appearances of Jesus Christ in the Gospels is the difficulty that his disciples, even his closest friends, had in recognizing him. They all saw the figure of a man, but most of them did not immediately know who he was. In the Gospel according to Luke, Jesus walked with two disciples for quite some time before they understood who he was. Mary Magdalene thought he was the gardener.

Matthew reports that some believed and some doubted. This is not altogether surprising, for all of them believed in the reality of death. They were convinced, as nearly all men are, that death, not life, is the final reality, and that life is not stronger than death. It is small wonder that they had a hard time believing and, when they did see him, did not recognize him.

Closely tied to the Resurrection is the Ascension of Jesus Christ. Just as in the Resurrection the bonds of sin and death were broken, so in the Ascension the bonds of space and time were broken. The belief was originally cast in a universe of levels rather than circles and cycles. Earth was below and heaven above. Later on, the notion of hell below was developed, but during the earliest of the biblical times the world was really a giant tent. The earth was the floor of the tent and the heavens were the sides and top. Above the circle of the tent's roof was heaven where God was enthroned.

Therefore, when the risen Christ broke the bonds of space and time, it was only natural in the biblical understanding that he should ascend into heaven. Today we would not accept the biblical way of looking at the universe, but it is imperative to understand what was meant in that conceptual framework. The risen Christ was no longer limited to the Palestine of the first century. In addition to being the risen Christ, he was also the universal Christ.

Much of popular religion in the Christian tradition has centered about a worship of Jesus. Indeed, there have been self-conscious "Jesus Only" movements in an attempt to get back to the simple carpenter of Nazareth. But all such movements have one fundamental drawback. They want to emulate the supposedly simple, itinerant rabbi of first century Palestine, unaware that such an emulation is a serious distortion of the gospel. The Christian faith centers in the Resurrection of Jesus Christ, and it is amply evident that there would have been no Christian faith apart from that Resurrection.

The notion of Jesus as a simple rabbi suffers from a second drawback. Modern man cannot go back into the first century. If the Christian faith is not pertinent to man in a modern, industrialized society, then it is not pertinent at all. The gospel cannot require that every believer retreat to the countryside and walk about in sandals. The heart of the biblical message is not the social and cultural conditions of the first century. It is the Resurrection of Jesus of Nazareth, and the reason that the Resurrection is pertinent to the twentieth century is that the risen Christ is more than a first century rabbi. In the Ascension he became a universal man.

Those who wish to emulate the simple carpenter of Galilee ultimately are trying to destroy him, for they will end up trying to render his death and sacrifice null and void. Man does not need one more moral exemplar so that he can work his way out of his malaise by trying once more to be better than he has been. An unseemly fascination with the life of Jesus apart from his Resurrection and Ascension brings only one more moral disillusionment. The function of the believer is certainly not to be more like Jesus or to ask what Jesus would do. The believer rather is to obey Jesus by following him in the twentieth century where, much to the surprise of nearly everyone, he is now living.

Another problem raised by the Resurrection of Jesus Christ is scientific. In terms of the strict, lockstep determinism of much of modern science, the Resurrection is generally regarded as an impossibility. Now, an impossibility is, strictly speaking, an event, or a possible event, that does not appear to fit into a rational scheme of things devised by man's mind. When something is considered impossible, the impossibility really means that according to someone's rational expectations that thing cannot happen. In other words, the notion of impossibility says as much about the one who thinks something impossible as it does about the possible occurrence of the supposed impossibility.

The problem is customarily couched in language about the laws of nature. But there are, strictly speaking, no such laws. God did not write down any laws of nature somewhere, along with the Ten Commandments. Isaac Newton did not discover them written on golden tablets in his backyard. They are, in fact, not laws at all. They are expectations based on past experience. One might say that at best they are predictions, and at worst enlightened guesses. They arise out of our observations of nature. From men's observations it is obvious that there is a certain regularity about things. This regularity is then called a law, and several regularities are called laws of nature. Modern man in his pragmatic atheism has become so preoccupied with his talent for prediction-based-on-observation that he has been led to the absurd conclusion that God could not act contrary to man's observations and predictions.

No one is about to say that the Resurrection of Jesus Christ is just another everyday event, not unlike many others. It is totally unique, but uniqueness and peculiarity do not necessarily imply impossibility. It would indeed be odd if God were to make a universe

so tied up in natural laws that he would eternally be
banished from it as a stranger and interloper. It seems
logical to assume that he would make a universe that
had a regularity so that man would not forever be
wandering around in a chaos of cataclysmic surprises.
The meaning of the first chapter of Genesis is that
God was bringing order out of chaos. But his ordering
of the chaos certainly made him no stranger to his
own world.

The ultimate purpose of the Crucifixion and Ressurrection was to restore God's creation to his original
intention. The purpose of redemption is a renewed
creation, and since creation was heading for destruction, any way of restoration would have been
unusual.

The concept of miracle has become almost useless
because it was based on an assumption about laws
of nature. A miracle was something supernatural
that contradicted the laws of nature. A miracle was
usually performed to show how great God was—as if
he needed to demonstrate his power and greatness.
But if there are no laws of nature, only observations
and predictions of high probability, then God's activity
in his creation is not a contradiction of creation but
a fulfillment or completion of it.

In these terms the Resurrection is not an impossibility. It is a totally unique possibility made probable
in view of God's intention to restore his creation by
redeeming it. He could have restored it by destroying
freedom and power, or he could have ignored it. Instead, he chose to restore his creation by redeeming
it, and to redeem it he had to break the powers that
were destroying it. That meant he had to become a
part of its destruction by suffering, being crucified,

and descending into its hell. It also meant that he had to break the power of destruction.

A belief in the Resurrection and Ascension of Jesus Christ hangs on the ability of the believer to make sense out of life. The historical evidence in the Gospels is not strong enough to compel belief in a person prone to disbelief. It really makes sense only when one has decided that life is stronger than death, that God is no stranger to his world, and that uniqueness does not imply impossibility. The Resurrection is the belief that Jesus Christ broke that which breaks men, that is, men's compulsion to find security through their own goodness and power. The Ascension is the belief that this reality is not confined to the first century, but is in fact a present reality in the lives of men who have responded to Jesus Christ with faith rather than goodness.

The Resurrection is the unique possibility of God's participation in his world to redeem it by conquering the forces that destroy it. While it may be contrary to man's observations and expectations, it is not alien to God's purposes; and it is contrary to man's observations and expectations only because man expects death rather than life. The Resurrection is a transformation from death to life, a redemption from disintegration that breaks the barriers of death.

9

The right hand of God the Father Almighty; From thence he shall come to judge the living and the dead

One of the difficulties with the Apostles' Creed is its metaphorical mixture. Literal and figurative statements are set side by side. Factual descriptions, such as "crucified, dead, and buried," are placed alongside such images as "sitteth at the right hand of God the Father Almighty." Some people of a more monolithic turn of mind, being uneasy with such a mix, either read the whole thing literally or throw it out. Part of the problem rests in an obvious truism. Modern man simply does not live in a world like that of the writers of the Apostles' Creed. Some moderns like to think that the old way was false and that the modern way is true, but this is arrogant nonsense. The old way of thinking was adequate to its time, and the new way may be adequate to its time. They are, however, neither true nor false. They simply explain things or they do not; and, if they do not, then a new way of expression must be found to fit the needs of the new time.

At the time of the composition of the Apostles' Creed a good many of the statements which are now taken metaphorically were taken literally. A prime example is the phrase, "sitteth at the right hand of God the Father Almighty." The men of the time believed in a three-storied universe, and heaven was literally supernatural—that is, above nature or earth.

Not only are we now forced to translate the ancient message from its three-level universe to one of cycles, spheres, and galaxies, but we are also forced to translate words and phrases reflecting a political situation now long gone. In ancient times monarchs, like modern men, could not be everywhere at once. Since they were not blessed—or cursed, if you will—with modern communications, they were limited when it came to keeping in contact with the various parts of their kingdom. To overcome this handicap they used a system of surrogates, men who were loyal enough to be totally trusted with the king's will. Whenever and wherever they went, these surrogates were received as the king himself would have been received. They were substitute sovereigns. A sign of their exalted status was their sitting at the right hand of the king. Having been elevated to such a status, they became, in fact, equal to the king in power and glory, even though their power and glory were derivative. Thus the writers of the Apostles' Creed, in using the phrase "sitteth at the right hand of God the Father Almighty" were taking a political image and using it to indicate their belief about Jesus Christ.

The image of the Son of God reflected the relationship of a father to a son and spoke of the inner dynamics of God in relationship to men. God the Father was the Creator, and God the Son the Redeemer. The image of the king and his surrogate spoke of God's mastery of history. The political image was aptly chosen, for the intention was political. Jesus Christ is the Judge and Redeemer of history—that is, of politics, the flow of civilization.

The advocates of a private religion generally postpone any historical activity on God's part to the last days when God will come to take his own and condemn the others. God's activity in history is largely a last minute rescue operation for his own. The social activists, on the other hand, use bits and snippets of Christian belief as a justification for their own philosophy of social change, grandly declaring that theirs is *the* Christian program for the future.

The difficulty with the private religionists is that they think of God mostly as an absentee landlord and see no particular pertinence of the gospel to the world God made and loved. The social activists generally suffer from a loss of historical memory, forgetting that nearly everyone in the history of western civilization since the first century has used Jesus Christ as a justification for a particular social program of one sort or another. Feudalism, free enterprise, liberation, slavery, democracy, monarchy, socialism have all been social gospels using Jesus Christ as a justification for their programs. The result of this sorry parade ought to lead one to a liberating skepticism, not an imprisoning commitment.

The belief that God, through Jesus Christ, is in control of history leads to two simple conclusions: a believer ought to participate with vitality in the flux and flow of history, and he should never commit himself with finality to any program.

However, the pragmatic atheism of modern man has inevitably caused a loss of a sense of destiny. Man's vision is generally so myopic that his self-generated sense of destiny seldom squares with the historical facts. The landscape of history is strewn with the wrecks of human machines of destiny whose meaning has burned out. The engines of meaning were not strong enough to move the weight of history's cargo. Absolute and divine-right monarchs, utopias, political programs, foolproof plans for peace, and wars to end wars are all parts of the wreckage.

The natural result of this high rate of casualty where such high hopes were entertained is an enervating pessimism. The self-generating designs of destiny have failed their believers, with the result that the believers have become either fanatics or cynics. A fanatic is a man who sees the inadequacy of his belief to explain his life and attempts to shore up that sagging belief with a supercharged commitment. A cynic is a man who rejects all belief because his particular belief has failed the test of time. Fanaticism is the attempt to make a belief credible by the intensity of the believer. Cynicism is a failure of nerve caused by the collapse of one's belief under the pressures of life.

The sense of destiny of modern, pragmatic atheists depends on elevating their private concerns and goals into a final reality—a kind of "worship of tribal deities". A man's ambition becomes the ultimate good. A nation's pride becomes its fountainhead of meaning. There is hardly a thing more fragile and less trustworthy than ambition or pride.

Paul characterized the Christian life as possessing three basic virtues—faith, hope, and love. Faith is essentially an experience rooted in the past. A child grows to have faith in his parents because of a history of love and trust. The experience of faith is not tied to a man's individual ambition or a nation's collective pride. It is rooted in a positive memory of experiences. If he believes that those examples of graciousness in his past were random events, he has seen them without the eyes of faith. If he sees them as a series of acts of God, then he has seen them with faith. Faith is a way of looking at life resulting from a profound awareness of God's graciousness. The author of the Epistle to the Hebrews describes it as the "assurance of things hoped for and the conviction of things not seen." (Heb. 11:1)

Hope, which is a sense of destiny, is a product of faith, as is love. Love is the capacity of a man to respond affirmatively to his experiences of others in spite of the conflicting ambiguity of life. A child loves his parents because he has first felt secure in their love. Before he can love them, he must have had faith in them. As he anticipates his life, he looks ahead with hope because of the positive experiences of his past.

The opposite of this is despair, the perception that nothing counts. It sometimes occurs in a woman who, when divorced, finds her life bereft of meaning because she previously pegged all her faith, hope, and love on a man who eventually repudiated her. It also occurs when a man loses the job to which he had given his whole life. It had been his past, his future, and his present. His job was the key to understanding his comings and goings.

The pathos is that men have made gods of perishable things, and, when the things perish, men perish with them. If a man gives his life to anything that might die, then the man is asking for his own death. To be sure, there can be a whole series of preliminary commitments and sources of meaning, but, if the preliminary is made final, death is the result. Isaiah said it well: "The grass withers, the flower fades, but the word of our God shall stand forever" (Isa. 40:8).

If the meanings run out with his own or his tribal destinies, then a man is faced with the necessity of faith *if* he wants to avoid the pitfalls of fanaticism and cynicism. There have been three traditional ways, other than chance, of perceiving a destiny. Some have believed that man's destiny is gradual improvement. Others have believed that it is a series of cycles in which history repeats itself. Still others have believed that it is a great drama in which men are the actors and God is the director and audience.

There is nothing in life or history which would lead anyone to a conclusive decision about the morality or amorality of life, much less about its purposefulness or lack of it. What leads a man to make a decision about these things comes from somewhere other than the data furnished by life and history, for the decision is an act of faith. The world seen as a chance and amoral world is as much an act of faith as the world seen as purposeful and moral. It all depends on where one stands, and the place a man stands reflects other realities than the brute facts of history.

One believes something because it helps him make sense out of life. Modern man moved from the three-storied universe of the ancients to a universe of galaxies because he could explain things better that way, and thus, a person's faith is rooted in the question of meaning.

Is a chance, amoral universe more sensible than a purposeful, moral one? One might well ask which of the two views would be more conducive to truth, beauty, and goodness. The advocates of a chance, amoral universe are compelled by their faith to account for the times of truth, beauty, and goodness. The advocates of a purposeful, moral universe are compelled also by their act of faith to account for the lies, ugliness, and evil in the world. It comes down to a hard decision: Is evil best explained in terms of goodness, or is goodness best explained in terms of evil?

The word "judge" is another one of the confusions of theology. In modern times, it has taken on a negative connotation, implying condemnation or an adverse judgment. Such an interpretation reflects more the temper of the age than the original meaning. A moment's reflection makes one aware that judgment can mean either a verdict of guilt or one of acquittal. It can mean either condemnation or redemption.

In the Old Testament the belief in the justice and judgments of God began with a dual concept—that if God were a just judge he would condemn the wicked and redeem the righteous. During the great social upheavals of the eighth, seventh, and sixth centuries B.C. in ancient Israel, when the rich, with the aid and comfort of the state, were systematically oppressing the poor, the prophets appealed to the justice of God and asked that the rich be condemned and the poor redeemed. As a matter of fact, their sense of righteous judgments was so strong that they ultimately made the word "righteousness" synonymous with the word "redemption."

When Jesus comes to judge the living and the dead, it is a judgment completing God's redemption of the world. It is the denouement of the plan revealed in his Crucifixion and Resurrection. In other words, the judgments of God are redemptive and not destructive. God sent his Son into the world "not to condemn the world, but that the world might be saved through him" (John 3:17).

The three traditional ways of looking at the universe in terms of purpose and morality have been a gradual improvement outlook, a repetitive cycle outlook, and a drama outlook. For those who maintain a moral estimate of the universe, the tendency is to swing between the gradual improvement theory and the repetitive cycle theory. The first is optimistic and the second pessimistic.

The gradual improvement theory has been the favorite of liberals because it generally supports their outlook on life. It holds that man is capable of moral improvements through education, sometimes through religious influences, and on occasion because of economic incentive. It has been called an "escalator" look at history, for it holds that over the centuries man's prospects have been gradually going up and that the future will be better than the present. It is a peculiarly modern view and an interesting gathering place for several modern forces. The first is the theory of evolution, which originally applied to biological matters but was then transferred to culture with the assumption that, as man was evolving physically, he was also improving spiritually or morally.

The belief in cultural evolution needed, in addition to a doctrine of evolution, an optimistic estimate of man's capacities for moral improvement. For support, it also needed a period of spectacular development in which civilization was so profoundly changed—apparently for the better—that the belief would be buttressed by the facts. Such a time was the eighteenth century, a time when the pump was invented, celestial navigation became a reliable instrument to be used in crossing the seas, and new continents were discovered.

The escalator theory of destiny is moral and it offers a positive hope. But it does not seem to square with the facts of history. It makes certain judgments of value which reveal the thinking of the evaluator more than the facts. The theory has fallen on hard times because of its inability to cope with the horrors of the twentieth century.

While the gradual improvement theory might be thought of as modern, the repetitive cycle theory is certainly classical. This theory holds that, although circumstances and appearances may change, the essence of things does not. It remains the same. Fundamentally, man does not change. His clothes, weapons of war, methods of healing, and all the accoutrements of his civilization will vary, but in the depth of his nature he is constant. This means that Shakespeare, Socrates, and Moses will have something to say to modern man; for, if man had improved, they would be less pertinent.

The repetitive cycle theory holds no hope for improvement in the future, for today is merely a rehearsal for tomorrow and a repeat performance of yesterday. But it is moral because man is able, from reading the past, to get a glimpse of what happens and to adjust himself to be as comfortable as possible in the present and future. He gains a certain amount of wisdom from the assurance that there is nothing new under the sun.

In the escalator theory of history, evil is subordinate to good, for good is gradually eradicating evil through the slow process of history. In the repetitive cycle or squirrel cage theory of history the forces of evil and good are about evenly balanced, for there is never any anticipation that one will conquer the other. The repetitive cycle theory is quite satisfactory in the way it explains the malaise of life, for life is ambiguous. However, it ends in resignation.

Some people have tried to combine the two into a theory which holds that gradually, through a series of slowly changing cycles (rather than circles), man is improving. This theory tries to take into account the obviously repetitive quality of human folly and adds a little hope that throughout all the convolutions of history, things get a little better. It suffers, however, from the same want of evidence as does the gradual improvement theory.

The repetitive cycle theory has a healthy realism about it, but it lacks a sense of spontaneity—an anticipation of life. The escalator theory lacks realism but offers spontaneity. The biblical theory of history is profoundly moral, for it sees history as the stage on which God is working out his plan.

From the biblical point of view, a sense of the spontaneity of life, an anticipation of the future, is rooted in the plan of God, not in the moral perfectibility of man. Rather than being optimistic about man, it is hopeful about God. It is as realistic as the repetitive cycle theory, holding no confidence in man's ability to improve himself. Indeed, it is so realistic that not even religious influences are seen as a possible source of moral improvement, for, no matter how long a man lives in God's grace, he still needs forgiveness. One of the paradoxical things about the Christian faith is that the longer a man lives in the context of God's graciousness, the less he believes in his own innate goodness.

The biblical sense of destiny is rooted in Jesus Christ. It affirms, on the one hand, the essential goodness of life and, on the other hand, the reality of evil. Evil is seen as a negation of the goodness. Evil is the force that corrupts goodness.

The biblical view is really quite simple. God's creation, which was made good, went askew through the corruption of its goodness by the goodness of man— that is, through man's attempt to find security. God acted decisively in Jesus Christ to break the power of human goodness which was destroying his creation. This he did in the Crucifixion, descent into hell, and the Resurrection. That event signaled the eventual outcome of man's history.

In every play there is a crisis point in which the final action of the play is foretold. A good many people miss the crisis point because they get too wrapped up in the details of the plot and the devices of the characters. There is usually a revelation in the play in which those who have eyes to see and ears to hear can get the point. The coming of Jesus Christ was that time of revelation in which, according to Paul, all the necessary wisdom and insight was given to the faithful to see the mystery of God's will for man (Eph. 1:10).

In his second inaugural address, Abraham Lincoln spoke of the purposes of God in history. Referring to the Scriptures, he claimed that these purposes were true and righteous altogether. It was that faith which gave Lincoln the capacity to endure the terrors of the Civil War. He required an utterly realistic assessment of man and a sense of destiny. He believed that he was, indeed, a part of a divine plan in which God was working out his will for his creation.

The failure of nerve of the twentieth century is the product of its enlightened pragmatic atheism, which made man optimistic, but without realism. To the contrary, the belief that Jesus Christ will come to judge the living and the dead recognizes that man's destiny is in God's hands; it allows man a realistic assessment of himself while maintaining his sense of destiny. As with Lincoln, it gives man the capacity to keep his nerve and thus renders man unfathomable to all the pragmatic atheists who still insist on living by their wits.

The Creed asserts that Jesus Christ sits at the right hand of God and thus is the master politician who will come to judge the living and the dead. As the master of politics, he comes as a profound challenge to any man who would live by his wits and virtues. This belief may make the believer a puzzlement to others, for he appears to be a realist with a sense of destiny. He has no illusion about anyone, including himself, but he can still hope, for he knows the world is a stage in which God's scenario is being acted out under God's direction.

10

The Holy Spirit

The Apostles' Creed appears to shift gears in its third and final part with a whole series of statements that at first appears to be a collection of afterthoughts, a pious potpourri thrown in just to cover the field and make everyone happy. It looks as if there is something for everyone once the Creed takes up the statement, "I believe in the Holy Spirit."

However, the Creed's ongoing attempt to focus on man is often undone at this point by repeating a naggingly bad habit found frequently among some believers. They like to refer to the Holy Spirit as an it. They may even capitalize the It, thus adding a touch of piety to their profanity. The Holy Spirit is not an "It" but a "He"—or "She." Yes, there may be something to be said for making the personal pronoun for God feminine now and then. The point is that the Spirit is not feminine or masculine, but personal. The Holy Spirit is not a substance, idea, or abstraction. He is a person!

A person is not necessarily a human being, for a person is a something that is aware of awareness, and by the act of self-awareness becomes not a something but a someone. A person, as distinguished from a non-person, is characterized by the ability to say "I," a fine personal pronoun which is neither feminine nor masculine.

Aside from the perversity of the act of rendering the Holy Spirit neuter, part of the problem rests with our language. In the first place, there is the linguistic habit of using the definite article "the" with the phrase Holy Spirit. One seldom, if ever, hears a Christian talking about "how Holy Spirit came into my life," although that same person might speak about "how Jesus came into my life." The definite article is deadly in that it objectifies the subject; it renders a person abstract.

The name printed on a formal Christmas greeting from "The Samuel Taylor Joneses" sounds like an institution, like Standard Oil of California. By contrast, one knows who "Sam and Susy" are; they are flesh and blood people, human beings, persons you can talk to. But it is hard to imagine confiding in "The Samuel Taylor Joneses," much less inviting them over to one's house and feeling comfortable about it.

"The" is a deadly article. It leeches all Sam Jones's humanity and leaves out Susy and the kids, not to speak of Roscoe, the golden retriever.

Just as "the" does not do much for Sam Jones, it does not do much for "the" Holy Spirit. It makes him an institution, an abstraction, or, worse yet, an idea. Although it would sound strange to one's ears at first, it might be a good idea just to drop the definite article.

The Creed implies that one should believe *in* "the" Holy Spirit, not believe *that* he exists. It is making a statement regarding a relationship, not asserting the existence of a substance. One does not believe in General Motors Corporation if he has his wits about him, although one might believe that it exists. The phrase "believe *in*" refers to a lively and living relationship and is more appropriately applied to persons, not institutions or corporations.

If the definite article is a liability, the word "holy" is not much help either. It is customarily used with things like Bible, table, and vessel. It is seldom used in reference to people, and when it is, it renders them remote. Not many people you know would be moved to invite "a holy man" for beer and barbecue. Holy men are usually found walking along lonely roads clothed in what appears to be old bedsheets, or being carried about on a sedan chair in pomp and circumstance by porters in fancy costume.

Literally, the word "holy" means "set apart". In the Bible it refers to messages from God, vessels used in worship, and prostitutes. Each one is set apart for a special use. Not many of the faithful are aware of this. They are likely to think that "holy" means especially good, mysterious, or remote from life.

The word "holy" in the phrase "the Holy Spirit" originally meant a special or unique relationship, and where that is the connotation the word is quite useful. One's relationship with God is different from one's relationship with another human being, no matter how precious and dear; it partakes of the same dynamics but its importance is without equal, it is set apart. In both the Old and New Testaments the word "spirit" first meant "wind." In its search for words from common experience to enlighten man's understanding of God, the biblical mind fastened on the word "wind." The most powerful forces the ancient nomads ever experienced were the desert siroccos blasting across the parched wastes and howling down the mountainsides and through the passes. They took the most powerful experience they knew in nature and used that word for God's presence.

Nowadays the word "spirit" has fallen on hard times. It has degenerated into such vacuous nonsense as "little spiritual talks" that usually lack force and pertinence and serve only to lull the lazy among the faithful. Sometimes it is used in statements like, "My, she is such a 'spiritual' person," by which a person devoid of visible connection with reality is commended for such a lack of connection.

The problem goes beyond language, for when the Creed says "in the Holy Spirit" it is using descriptive words, not names. The word "God" is not a name, strictly speaking, though in tandem with the word "Father" it has for most people become a name. Actually, the word "Father" is descriptive, but in general usage it has become functionally a name. When a child calls his father "Daddy," the word has become a name. In the Lord's Prayer the word "Father" is also used much like a name.

However, the words "holy" and "spirit" have never developed the same sense of intimacy. They remain descriptions of a function, and thus become abstractions or ideas. In the seventeenth chapter of John, Jesus refers to Holy Spirit as Comforter, Counselor, or Advocate. The Greek word is Paraclete. Its original verbal form literally meant "to be called to one's side," to stand beside someone as a comforter, aide, helper, and advocate. It would seem that Jesus' reference to Holy Spirit as Paraclete is more useful than the phrase in the Creed.

One of the sad things about the Christian faith is that it often gets bogged down in its own language—or sidetracked into a whole series of misunderstandings and irrelevancies. The phrase "the Holy Spirit" has often sent the faithful down blind alleys of meaning and into culs-de-sac of nonsense. Fundamentally, the phrase refers to God's abiding presence in a man's life, the continual awareness that God is present even when one feels him absent. As a matter of fact, one of the great surprises of the Christian experience is that God's presence is known in man's feelings of his absence as well as in man's feelings of his presence. The darkness of the shadow of his hand is like the radiance of his light in that both are evidences of his abiding presence.

One of the phrases used in Matthew for referring to Jesus Christ occurs in the birth narrative. Jesus is called Immanuel, God with us. The statement "God with us" has twin meanings. First, it means that God is not antagonistic to man but favorable to him. Second, and derivatively, it means that because God is *for* man he also abides *with* him; he does not come as a stranger and sojourner in man's life but as a companion, an abiding presence.

It is not accidental that the Creed focuses on the Holy Spirit only after having spoken of God the Father and Jesus Christ, for the Holy Spirit comes from the Father and the Son. According to classical Christian belief, God the Father sent the Son to redeem that world which the Father had made through the Son, and once the Son had accomplished his work of redemption, then the Father and the Son sent the Holy Spirit as the continuing presence of God.

Perhaps the best way to explain it is with reference to prayer. A man prays to God the Father. He is able to pray, to approach God, because Jesus Christ reconciled him to God the Father. He is helped in his prayers through the Holy Spirit. The same dynamics can be seen taking place with a small child and his mother. The child may have had an altercation with his mother and, being afraid to come to her, finds that she is coming to him looking for a reconciliation. As he stumbles for words, his mother helps him to find himself and express himself to her. Because of her love for the child, she is simultaneously his judge, his reconciler, and his helper. She is three persons to him in his communion with her, and without those three persons he really could never have a satisfactory communion with her.

In addition to the image of prayer, the image of communication is useful. If God really loves man and wants to reveal himself to man, then He has to get the message across. God the Father initiates the revelation by sending his Son, and the Son *is* the revelation: the content of the revelation is God himself. The Holy Spirit is the enabler by whom man is helped to understand the message. God not only speaks to man, he becomes the content of the message, and he helps man understand the meaning of the message.

The Holy Spirit gives man the capacity to respond in faith to God's gracious promises of life, to love in spite of life's ambiguities, and to hope that God's graciousness will finally triumph over man's goodness. If the Creed had stopped with the revelation of Jesus Christ, then it would have left out the one who would make that revelation real. A believer would be left with ideas and history, but no abiding presence in his life.

It is easier to dissect belief and investigate history than it is to explain experience, but the third part of the Apostles' Creed focuses on experience. This section, like the others, begins "believe in" and not "believe that." Unlike the others, however, it begins, after the initial statement, to speak directly about man. In the first two parts of the Creed all of the statements about God the Father and God the Son can be interpreted as being also statements about man and questions about man's life. But once this section on the Holy Spirit begins, the discourse about man is no longer indirect.

One of the constant problems facing a believer is the means by which the Holy Spirit makes himself known, and how one experiences His presence. If, in fact, the heart of religious experience is not ideas, morals, or emotions but a relationship, then how does that relationship take place? Believers respond to that question in various ways. Some believe that God makes his presence known through objects and things, such as the sacraments, holy objects and vessels, sometimes even sticks and stones. At first, this concept of objectification strikes one as somewhat primitive but, like nearly all things, it has an element of truth. Certain objects in a man's life do remind him of other unseen realities—he wears a wedding ring to remind himself of his marriage. The problem with objects and things is that most men have a tendency to think that God is really present in the object—the object *is* the presence. Some tribes actually think that their deity is in the stone. Some Christians act as if the family Bible is an inherently holy object with overtones of God's presence. If a person thinks that the object is a symbol of God's presence, then the object serves a useful purpose. But if it becomes confused with the presence itself, then the symbol becomes demonic and destructive. Paul Tillich has observed that symbols are useful only if they are transparent to the reality to which they point.

While some people find God in objects, others think in terms of the subjectification of the presence of God in the heart of the believer. God is present when the believer's heart is "strangely warmed." Perhaps the most vivid example of this approach is found in the emotional conversions of which much of American Protestantism is so fond. The emotions of the heart which are the symbols and signs of God's presence can run all the way from the stark fire and brimstone terror of revival meetings to the exaggerated sentimentality found in the hearts of middle-aged matrons upon entering a softly lit house of worship.

While the first response is an attempt to objectify God's presence in external symbols, the second is an attempt to subjectify God's presence in terms of human emotion. The danger of the second attempt is that if God is thought to be available through our emotions, then certain emotions will be thought to guarantee the presence of God. The consequence might well be artificially induced emotions.

It is obvious that when God encounters a person, the person's emotions are affected, but because people's emotions are as varied as are people, it is impossible to establish a catalog of acceptable emotions. Anger may be as sure a sign of God's presence as happiness. The fleeting and transitory nature of emotions make them poor indicators, and they surely are inadequate gauges of God's presence.

Another means traditionally regarded by the faithful as assuring God's presence is the presentation of his message. God becomes known to mankind through words spoken by people about God. In certain types of Protestantism this idea is dominant, as evidenced by an emphasis on preaching. The presence of God is objectified in "correct" theology, which tests and verifies the adequacy of the sermonic theology.

Not infrequently one hears some pious soul affirm that someone else's prayers did not get beyond the roof because they were not "correct" or "acceptable to God." This is a prime example of the belief that God's presence comes through the accuracy of ideas, and it places a profound handicap on God's activity among men; for if he is present only among those with "acceptable ideas," he probably will be confined to a very narrow circle of believers indeed.

Each one of these traditional ways of thinking about God's presence misses the point. Those who think that God is present in objects finally reduce the abiding presence of God to a mechanical toy which can be manipulated by tinkering with the parts. Those who insist on emotions as a sign of his presence suffer from the consequences of mistaking means and responses. Emotions are the varied human responses to events, but they are not means by which an experience takes place. (Indeed, one can even experience another person without much emotion.) Those who feel that the presence of God is dependent upon words must realize that words, although capable of being symbols pointing to a reality beyond themselves, can also be demonic if they become substitutes for reality. There are no "correct" phrases for invoking God's presence.

The rest of the Creed begins to answer the question regarding the means of assuring God's presence, for once a person says that he believes in God's presence in his life, then the inevitable question arises as to how this relationship is maintained. The phrases "the holy catholic church" and "the communion of saints" are the beginnings of the answer.

11

The Holy Catholic Church,
the Communion of Saints

There is a widespread feeling that the church may not be necessary. If religion is an individual matter, the argument runs, then one might well question why it should be organized. Part of the current malaise is the fault of the church itself. The conflicting claims of the various denominations and confessions make one wonder if the squabbling does not mute the sound of the church's message. If five or six people clamor that they have a corner on the truth and none of them agrees with any of the others, the average, sensible man is tempted to walk away from the fracas.

However, behind and beyond the verbal confusion of the church's assessment of itself, there is another issue far more fundamental, the issue of the person and the community. Where does a man find himself in his society? What is the relationship between his independence and freedom on the one hand and the claims of the community on the other hand? Can a man survive, much less flourish, sustained only by his own resources?

The biblical witness is quite clear. In its wrestling with the issue the question is not posed in an either/or fashion. Paul uses the image of the church as the body of Christ in which Christ is the head and believers are its members. The uniqueness of the believers is not achieved in isolation but in relationship.

Originally, the chief symbol of this unity in diversity was a joyous meal in which the believers were gathered together to remember the sacrifice of the cross, to celebrate the reality of the presence of the risen Christ, and to anticipate his eventual cosmic triumph. This meal has been variously designated in the history of the church as the Eucharist, Holy Communion, and the Lord's Supper.

Unfortunately, what was intended as a symbol of unity has in fact become a means of disunity, for the conflicting claims of the denominations and confessions often revolve around the pivot of the sacred meal. The scandal is that the church often resembles a kitchen fight in which the cooks are quarreling over the recipes with the result that the guests are reluctant to sit down to the meal together. It is agreed that the presence of the risen Christ is associated with the Lord's Supper. The differences surface when one begins to describe the means by which he makes his presence known among the faithful.

This sorry plight indicates something amiss. In the first place, Christ's presence has been treated as if he were a substance, rather than a person. The doctrine suffers from the "itness" often associated with the Holy Spirit, for if the Holy Spirit is an it, a neuter, then his presence, or its presence, would be impersonal.

The real issue is the nature of the Christian faith. Is it a status, a matter of being in a "state of grace"? Is it pious feelings? Right actions? If it is any one of these things, then some variation of the traditional doctrines of the Lord's Supper or Eucharist would do just fine. However, if one believes that the heart of the Christian faith is a personal relationship with God in Jesus Christ, then the whole thing is turned around.

After a relationship is initiated there are means by which it is betokened, and these means are generally called symbols. They include such things as words, ideas, gestures, even sticks and stones, mementos and diamonds, and all manner of human activity. A relationship is in deep trouble, however, when people assume that the symbols of the relationship equal the relationship itself.

The traditional debate has often revolved around which church had a corner on Christ. The church which celebrates the Eucharist or the Lord's Supper under the "right" concepts and in the "right" way is assured of Jesus Christ's presence. This consequence is, of course, a pious blasphemy. John 3:7-10 suggests that the Holy Spirit moves when and where he wills, and the machinations of men cannot assure his presence or his absence.

The phrase "means of grace"—used in referring to word and sacraments—is itself a mechanical idea, for it assumes that God's grace is a substance which can be passed along in a sort of hydraulic system. Also, one sometimes hears metaphors alluding to electric circuitry and wind tunnels. God's grace does not have means or channels, for it is not an it, a substance. God's attitude toward man is conveyed by persons using symbols, not by organizations using circuits.

Since the Christian faith is a personal relationship with God in Jesus Christ, the symbols of that relationship are personal. During the Reformation of the sixteenth century one of the crucial points raised by Martin Luther and John Calvin was the doctrine of the priesthood of all believers. Their quarrel with the Roman Church was not that the Roman Church had priests; it was that they did not have enough of them. The Roman Catholics had selected certain of the faithful as priests while Luther and Calvin thought that all believers should be priests.

A priest is one who mediates between God and man and represents man before God. The point of the Reformers was that every believer was a priest to his fellow believers. They did not quarrel with the notion that there ought to be priests; they wanted to spread the function around among all the faithful.

If the Christian faith is a personal relationship with God in Jesus Christ, then the priest is one who mediates that relationship through his relationship with his fellow believers. The Reformers wanted to make that function the task of every believer so that the fellowship of the church would be the means of grace, so that the communion of saints (believers) would be the way that the gracious presence of God is expressed. It is through persons that God communicates himself to men. The sacraments and ordinances of the church are not the means of grace. People are. The sacraments and ordinances are signs of a presence already made known through the communion of saints.

The statement "believe in" does not refer to the phrases "holy catholic church" and "communion of saints." It refers to the Holy Spirit in whom a person believes because he is a child of God. Belief refers to a quality of relationship, not to an idea. However, the phrases that pile up in a row after the statement of belief in the Holy Spirit are not "believed in," as it were. They are not the relationship, but the means of the relationship.

That is what is wrong with saying that prayer has power. Prayer has no power. God does. God's power comes through the prayer—and sometimes even in spite of the prayer—but the prayer does not have power. A similar problem is found in the statement about the power of faith. Faith has no power. God does, and God may manifest his power through a person of faith. But the faith itself is not the source of the power. God is.

The word "church" originally came from the verb "to call out," a word used in the cities throughout the Roman Empire to denote the gatherings of citizens of a city who had been called out from the general populace to conduct the business of the city. It was an apt word for the gathering of the faithful because it could be used to denote the belief that God had called the church out from the world to worship and serve him, to conduct the business of the acts of God.

In Matt. 18:20 Jesus promised to be among the faithful wherever two or three of them were gathered in his name. Paul constantly refers to the church as the body of Christ, and goes on to say that Christ is the head of the body and believers are members of the body. The implication is quite strong that one cannot function apart from the body, for a hand cut off is no longer a hand but a piece of dead flesh. In John 15 Jesus uses a similar analogy. He calls himself the vine, the Father the vinedresser, and the believers the branches of the vine.

These references all point to a notion that believers are interdependent members of a community. This simple reality of the church as a community of be-

107

lievers, all of whom are priests of God's presence to each other, is often confused with what one might call the institutional church. The institutional church refers to all the paraphernalia, both pious and impious, that are used to keep the community going. It refers to ministers, priests, bishops, superintendents, synods, dioceses, bureaus, agencies, publishing houses, Sunday schools, parochial schools, and the whole panoply of organizations and systems used to carry out the purpose and work of the church. It might be pointed out that when the average person uses the word "church" he is probably referring to the institutional church.

In the modern era there has been considerable anti-institutional feeling—easily justified since institutions, however necessary, are often corrupt. They become corrupt when they make arrogant claims. The institutional church has not been altogether above reproach in this respect. But the institutional church is merely the *means* by which the community of faith organizes itself to nurture itself and communicate the message of the gospel to all men. As such, it is subject to all the usual human imperfections.

Anyone who has been in the church inevitably asks himself the question: Is the church really necessary? If one believes that God makes himself known and relates to people through people, then a community of faith is necessary. If that community of faith wants to do an effective job, then it has to organize itself in the most efficient way possible to nurture itself and spread the gospel.

However, the question is immediately raised about the various types of church organization. There is an endless supply of church organizational tables, and each one claims some type of biblical sanction for doing things its own way. While there may be some truth to the belief that the church in the New Testament organized itself in a certain way, there is also truth to the notion that the system of organization reflected the times as much as it did the gospel. For instance, it would be very hard, if not impossible, to fit Paul into any modern ecclesiastical system. He was an itinerant genius living off of occasional gifts and earnings. and subject only in a voluntary way to ecclesiastical authorities, that is, what ecclesiastical authorities there were.

It is not without coincidence that an episcopal or hierarchical system of church government grew up in a time of emperors, kings, and monarchs. It is a system in which the bishops have the power and delegate it downward. Also, it is not surprising that congregational and presbyterian systems of government would arise in the modern era since they closely resemble democracies and republics. Finally, it should not be surprising that the episcopal systems are taking on presbyterian modifications and that some congregational systems are adopting presbyterian accoutrements. This is the age of the representative democracy or republic, and it would be strange indeed to find the church unaffected by the predominant organizational systems.

One cannot say that any system of government is the appropriate skeletal structure for the body of Christ. There are systems that work, systems that work poorly, and systems that do not work at all. It is impossible to say that God's presence is tied to a particular system of organization. He makes himself known through the communion of believers, not the means by which the believers organize themselves.

It is almost universally accepted that the Lord's Supper or Eucharist is the central act of the church's life and is a celebration of exceptional importance. But the claim presents a problem to us today. The problem is very simple. Jesus promised that he would abide through his Holy Spirit among the faithful gathered in his name. But how would he do it? If one reflects on his own Christian experience, it soon becomes apparent that Jesus Christ has overtaken one's life through the influence of others, that is, through the priesthood of believers. The faith is communicated personally.

Man loves symbols. He lives by symbols. They are his most significant means of communication. Communication is vital to a relationship, because relationship is an intangible built upon faith and trust. The Word and the Sacraments, traditional Protestant signs of the true church, are signs of a vital and living relationship—*if* the relationship is there. If it is not, the signs may still exist. In the same way, words of endearment, gestures of affection, and relations of intimacy occur continually without either grace or faith. They are valid only if they are symbols of a reality already present, a living and loving relationship.

The Lord's Supper is special because, like all important means of celebration, it enlivens the relationship. A dinner with old friends sometimes enlivens a relationship which one has begun to take for granted. The relationship is not the same thing as the dinner, but the dinner has the ability to make one aware of what is already there. The Lord's Supper is not a means of assuring the presence of Jesus Christ in the church through the Holy Spirit. Instead it makes believers aware that he is already present, always has been, and always will be.

Karl Rahner, one of the great contemporary Roman Catholic theologians, in wrestling with the problem of the church, has stated that the church has sacraments only because it is first of all *the* fundamental sacrament. What he means is that the church is the means by which God's presence abides among men. This belief is the problem of the church, for it is making a claim, not of privilege, but of responsibility for its own life.

12

The Forgiveness of sins

Every statement made about man's relationship to God is a two-edged sword, for when a man says something about God, he is inadvertantly saying something about himself. Also, when he says something about himself, he is inadvertantly saying something about his perceptions of God. One of the most effective ways to find out what a man believes about God is to find out what he believes about himself.

The last three phrases in the Apostles' Creed purport to be statements about the quality of the Christian life, but they are just the tips of doctrinal icebergs. In the phrase "the forgiveness of sins" there are two focuses, the forgiveness of God and the sins of man, and one cannot be understood apart from the other.

In addition to the two-edged quality of theological statements, one has to realize that frequently the phrases are metaphorical rather than literal. This realization is threatening to some, for they fear it will lead to a watering down of the integrity of the faith. While that may be a danger, metaphorical statements may also be liberating in that they allow for diversity and breadth of understanding. For instance, the phrase "forgiveness of sins" is but one of several phrases found in the Bible which point to the believer's quality of life.

Many people become confused concerning metaphorical statements, assuming that if a statement is not literal it is not true. This would, of course, nullify the parables of Jesus Christ. The validity of the parable does not depend upon its historical accuracy, for the parables were cut out of the whole cloth of man's life. The images used in the Bible for the relationship between God and man are not esoteric theological words designed to confound the faithful; they are images from everyday life used to illustrate the quality of the relationship.

A relationship cannot be reduced to a narrow definition, but it can be variously illustrated. The images used in the Bible are verbal pictures illustrating the relationship. Each image says two things about man: what he is and what he could be. Each image illustrates his actuality and his potential. If one considers the implications of these images, one can begin to see the richness of biblical imagery.

The basic idea of the word "sin" in the New Testament is that of missing the mark. The term comes from the imagery of the archer. It refers to a misspent life, the giving of oneself and all his energies not so much in dissolute behavior as into a scheme of life that missed the point. Phrases such as "good try" and "she meant well" refer to the same experience.

Sin has something of that quality. It is a man's attempt to make sense out of his life by making something of himself. Most men categorize human acts as good or bad. Goodness and badness are variously defined by different societies. Generally, the good is defined by the prevailing group as those patterns of behavior that sustain and support its interests, while the bad is simply that which adversely affects its interests.

In militaristic societies, the virtues are martial and the vices peaceful. In capitalistic societies, the virtues are aggressive and the vices placid. In rural societies, the virtues are agricultural and the vices urban. The virtues are those patterns of behavior by which people attempt to understand the meaning of their lives. Oddly enough, so are the vices. In a society which values chastity a woman of loose virtue is seeking meaning through a counter virtue; she seeks meaning by way of defiance rather than acquiescence. The young rebel, the dropout, the angry protester defying conventions are using the customary vices and turning them into rebellious virtues in their search for meaning. They achieve a stature of sorts by defying the conventions, while their conforming associates achieve stature by obeying them. The defiant are called bad and the conforming good. Vice and virtue are oddly alike. They can both be used to "make it" spiritually, to prove one's self-worth.

What annoys establishment people is not so much the defiance of the rebels as their self-righteousness. The pot smokers and acid droppers always accompany their defiance with a great deal of verbiage about the hypocrisy and phoniness of middle-class citizens. They abuse their elders for traits they exhibit themselves.

The dynamics of sin are seldom those which one sees and hears, for the human problem is not essentially *what* a man does but *why* he does it. It is important to put band-aids on the wounds of the human spirit, but one cannot stop there. It is important that an alcoholic stop drinking, but the act of stopping, heroic as it might be, is only a prelude to redemption.

The dynamics of human life are not a matter of doing good things and avoiding bad things. The origins of sin rest within the human heart—in man's attempt to live as though God were not, to build up some sort of security, some province of meaning for himself. The customary definition of sin as something bad ignores the real problem, which is not what a man does but why he does it. In classical theology this more fundamental problem is referred to by the term "original sin." The man and the woman in the Garden of Eden are not historical creatures who have passed their faults on genetically down through the generations. They are paradigms of human malaise. They are, as it were, everyman. Vice and virtue are alike, for they are both forms of sin.

A society that speaks of "underachievers" and "overachievers" is one that assumes a system of virtue based on justification-by-achievement; and ironically its system of vice is, as often as not, based on condemnation-by-defiance. If the self credit system fails, then one has only to "drop out." There are a great many people in a society of achievement who want to stop the world so that they can get off.

In these terms sin is the attempt to justify one's life, to make good, to achieve so that one can prove oneself worthy. The man and the woman wanted to be like God and sought justification by works; they tried to make it on their own, without faith in God. This is sin because it is a repudiation of God.

A man may derive his sense of significance from those who have loved him or from his achievements. One of the reasons that there is so much loneliness in a society of achievement is that one is forced into the lonely posture of going it alone. The more precarious one's position becomes, the greater the temptation to prove oneself—hence, the greater the estrangement and isolation. Justification by grace through faith implies a need for others, and immediately and ultimately a need for God's gracious disposition.

A man can think himself important by what he does, by who has loved him, and by where he hopes to go. The first requires faith in the merit of what he does from day to day. The second requires faith in the source of the love, and the third requires faith in the importance of his destiny. Justification by grace through faith is the spiritual health, the inner vitality, that comes from knowing one's everlasting significance in Jesus Christ. Not only is the cross a sign of the misery of man, it is also a sign of God's ultimate estimate of man's worth. Man's sin was so great that it demanded the sacrifice of Jesus Christ, but God's regard for man was so great that it demanded God pay the price of man's redemption.

The system of achievement breeds an ethic of competition, for achievement assumes some standard of judgment against which one can measure himself. Competition can either be against an objective standard, such as not having sexual intercourse before marriage; against others, such as grade point averages in school; or against oneself, such as topping last year's production quota. All of these isolate a man. If one avoids sexual entanglements before marriage, then one feels ethically superior to those who do not. The conventional image of a Christian is often that of a moral prig who thinks himself pure, and therefore better than others.

One of the loneliest persons in school is often the student who gets all the A's—he sets himself apart by his achievement. If his self-esteem hangs on achievement, then for him the school becomes not so much a community of knowledge in which students and faculty together share the joy of learning as a collection of loners, each trying to make it by bettering the others in the rat race for excellence.

The image of reconciliation used by Paul is one of the most relevant for modern society. Originally it referred to the estrangement between Jew and Gentile and between God and man. His argument is very simple: As men are reconciled to God, they are reconciled to each other (Eph. 2:11-22). The ethical systems of various cultures are generally self-serving; and when people of various cultures clash, it is, as often as not, the systems of ethics or values that are clashing. If a man achieves merit through mastery of a system of values, then an alien system of values is an immediate threat to his sense of worth.

One of the objections to an ethic of relationship is that it deprives a man of motivation. The reply is that it releases energy rather than driving a man through fear to prove himself. Does a student learn best when he is compelled by fear to prove himself? Or when he wants to learn for the sheer joy of knowledge? The answer is obvious.

The inner turmoil found in isolation and estrangement is the focal point of another biblical image. The ideas of cleanness and uncleanness in the Bible are baffling for modern man. Originally they referred to ceremonial pollution, a kind of ritual acceptability or unacceptability. Eventually, they came to refer to an inner wholeness which made a person clean, inner disintegration being uncleanness.

In the fifteenth chapter of Matthew Jesus speaks of

the inner disintegration of uncleanness. Essentially, it is the hypocrisy of achievement; for, if a man is to "make it" morally, he must live an illusion, the illusion being that he has it made. As the Jew had found at the time of Jesus Christ, no one could ever fulfill all the law's demands. This required, then, the art of hypocrisy if one was to survive since the system did not allow for mercy. Hypocrisy is the ruse by which those who cannot live by their system of achievement, but cannot repudiate the system, deceive themselves and others into thinking that they have indeed succeeded. This is the uncleanness, the internal disintegration which comes from living a lie.

God makes clean by his message of mercy. One of the remarkable things about the forgiveness of sin is the resulting ability to face up to life. If a person's self-esteem does not hang on total success, then he can afford to face his failures. If his significance does not stem from his goodness, then he can afford the luxury of the confession of his sins. The foundation of hypocrisy is forever destroyed in a person's life if he is once convinced that his sickness is not a shame.

If a person is made clean, it means that he no longer has to strive for achievement. Christian ethics assumes that before one begins he has already made it. He does not have to strive to prove anything, much less prove himself. Christian ethics starts where other ethical systems end—a man has it made even before he tries.

If this is the case, he is free from the burden of proof, from the sapping of his energy in a compulsion to establish himself. He is free to accomplish and to enjoy his relationships because his self-esteem does not hang on these things. In modern society even relationships have become a means of achievement.

People customarily wonder if they are "relating well" —as if relating were an activity pursued individually. A person does not just relate; he relates *to* someone. And if he considers his ability to relate to someone as an achievement, then he has ceased to relate to anyone at all.

Oddly enough, this may mean that those who ordinarily think of themselves as the greatest "relaters" may indeed have no relationships at all, for they think of a relationship more as an achievement than as a gift. They are "plastic personalities." Relationships are not achievements; to need someone else and to trust in him is to realize that achievements have failed. When a man has conquered all there is to conquer and then recognizes that he is alone, he has begun to develop the capacity for a relationship. Hypocrisy, which is the salve for failure in a system of achievement, is the attempt to appear *as if* one loves and trusts while in fact still living a lie.

The further one proceeds along the course of self-justifying achievement, estranged competition, and salving hypocrisy, the deeper one becomes entrenched in a system from which there is no escape. If one fails in the system of achievement, the only way out is to try harder. If one succeeds, he has to try harder for an even greater success, so that no matter whether a man fails or succeeds he is always goaded on to greater achievement. If a mile runner breaks the world record after years of trying, he has two alternatives—keep trying to break his own record or drop out of the race. The pathos is that, no matter what he does, he is trapped. He can keep at it the rest of his life or he can retire; but whichever he does he is still the man who won the race. A mile runner who does not win the world record can keep on trying or quit, but then he will always understand himself as the one who did not win or could not win. Defined by his achievement —or lack of it—he remains the captive of the achievement system.

Jesus Christ is called the Savior, which means that he can deliver people from their misery and despair. He saves people from their sins. This customarily is thought of as saving them from their misdeeds, but that is far wide of the mark. More often than one would care to admit the Christian faith has been used to support and buttress the prevailing system of achievement rather than liberating people from it. The customary idea of saving people from sin means to make them better in terms of the prevailing morality. Saving in the biblical faith means delivering them from the death grip of the prevailing morality.

Jesus Christ is Savior because he offers a way out. He submitted himself to the prevailing system of goodness and broke it. The morality of the believer is one of acceptance, not achievement. God reached across the chasm of space and time and in Jesus Christ opened an avenue of salvation, a way out of the system of achievement, estrangement, and hypocrisy.

Closely akin to the image of salvation is that of redemption. It originally meant to buy back someone or something. The implication was that the one needing redemption was in bondage to someone else. In medieval theology the bondage was to the devil. Generally, redemption from bondage came at a price. The theory was that in Jesus Christ God paid to the devil the price for the redemption of man, which meant, of course, that in an odd way God paid the devil his due.

The idea is at first ridiculous and repugnant until one realizes what it means—that God took the world seriously! He would not betray his creation by the fiat of goodness; rather he affirmed it in a sacrifice of redemption. If the system of evil is the indirect creation of God through his creation of its possibility, then he is responsible for it. Paying the price meant that God would not wipe out the possibility of goodness while wiping out the actuality of evil.

For most people, Christian ethics does not mean liberation but imprisonment. The biblical image holds that the ethics of *achievement* is bondage. Jesus Christ is the means of liberation. His sacrifice is the price of freedom, man's freedom to live no longer by the canons of goodness but of graciousness.

Jesus Christ broke the power of the system of achievement by submitting himself to the system in the form of Roman law and Jewish religion—the classic examples of the corruption of human goodness. The contest was between the graciousness of God and the goodness of man, and in the Resurrection the graciousness of God triumphed.

The ultimate question with respect to forgiveness of sins is whether man will look at himself as do the human institutions of goodness, or in terms of the gospel of Jesus Christ. The forgiveness of sins says that the thing most men strive for is in fact a gift, that the place most men hope to get is where the believer already is, and that liberation from the system of achievement requires one simple and awful step: a man must trust no longer in his own capacity to make something of himself but in the grace of God, believing that God has already made something of him in the Crucifixion and Resurrection of Christ.

The purpose of the forgiveness of sins is not to make good people out of bad people. It is to liberate persons from the imprisonment of human goodness so they can live graciously in terms of Jesus Christ. The result is a life lived out of God's love rather than out of man's achievement.

13

The Resurrection of the body,
And the Life everlasting

The Christian church is laden with problems that
would bury most institutions. It erects vast educa-
tional buildings and then uses them once a week. Its
method of operation is often chaotic. It is locked into
antique ways of doing things, thinking that preservation of the antiques is preservation of the ancient
faith. One of its gravest problems, however, is its language.

For the most part, biblical language was originally
cast in a rural environment, and the world, at least
the western world, has ceased to be largely rural. The
gospel first came on the scene in the times of emperors and kings, but most moderns picture royalty in
quaint and ceremonial roles. When men of absolute
power arise, they are generally regarded with horror
and repulsion. So in addition to having the liability of
agricultural language in an industrial civilization, the
church's political language is of an era now happily
thought bygone.

Supposedly, the greatest mark of distinction between the biblical times and the present is that the
biblical was religious and the present is secular. But

even the religious people today are secular. "Secular" means thinking of life in terms of the present rather than the hereafter. Religious man sees his present life in terms of eternity, and secular man, if he believes in eternity, sees his life as an extension of the present. Secular men are different from atheists, either practical or theoretical; they are very theistic, that is, they have all sorts of gods.

Thus the church is confronted with a very simple problem. Can it translate a message fundamentally set within the framework of a supposedly religious outlook into a secular milieu? The liberals often as not launch into the task with verve and vitality; they busy themselves "demythologizing" the Christian message—by which they mean to rid it of its religious and other-worldly character and recast it in modern, secular terms. The conservatives often try to keep both the vessels of antiquity and the ancient message, thinking that both are somehow inextricably tied together; and to a degree they are right.

Ironically, the ancients were not that religious, and modern man is certainly not that secular. The Bible itself is a peculiarly practical book dealing with all manner of this-worldly situations. The heart and core of the book is found in the belief that God did not remain in eternity but became a part of time. He became a man. The enfleshment of God makes the Bible a very this-worldly book.

Modern man has a way of getting caught up in transcendent causes and final solutions, as if his problems could be solved once and for all by a belief, a scheme, and even a system. The beliefs that have been regularly thought to be the most "religious" are the resurrection of the body and the life everlasting. It is important to realize that when the Creed speaks of these matters it is not just saying something that people often think is the essence of religious belief anyway —it does not mention the "immortality of the soul," which is a peculiarly religious idea.

Part of the misunderstanding on this score arises from the fact that the gospel was originally cast in Hebraic forms of thought, and its first extensive translation occurred when that message was carried into the Graeco-Roman world. Although the Romans had conquered the Mediterranean basin and Europe politically and militarily, the Greeks had conquered much of that same territory culturally. Greek was the *lingua franca* of the time; it was the language of commerce and culture. Thus, when the gospel was preached in the Mediterranean area and Europe, it was put in Greek terms.

The Greeks were a more religious people than the Hebrews. The early Hebrews, such as Moses and the prophets, did not even believe in an afterlife. The Greeks, through Persian influences, had developed an elaborate set of ideas regarding life after death. They had centered their views around a peculiar idea which held that man was a composite of two parts, soul and body. The soul was spiritual and immortal, and the body was fleshly and mortal. By this they meant that the soul in and of itself would not die; it was inherently divine and thus immortal. When the body of flesh died, the immortal soul would leave its captivity in the body and gain its eternal freedom.

Many early Christians confused this Greek belief with the biblical one and that confusion has remained throughout Christian history, with the result that most people think the immortality of the soul is a Christian doctrine. It is not, for in the first place the biblical mind was impressed with the mortality of man, and secondly, it did not split man into a duality of soul and body.

In the second creation story the Lord God made man from the dust of the earth, much as he would make a mud pie, then breathed into that mass of dust the breath of life—the result was a living being. Man was not given a soul; he came alive (Gen. 2:7).

When God made man, he did not invest man with deity; rather he created man in his image. The word "image" does not mean "of the same essence." It originally meant shadow. The idea was that man had a relationship of dependency on God. One of the last things that would cross the ancient Hebraic mind was that man was possessed of a little divinity, a spark of God.

One of the things about man that impressed the Hebraic mind most of all was his frailty. He was of the dust and would return to the dust. There is no evidence that the Hebrew believed, as did the Greek, that man had a divine soul within him. Rather man was made of dust, was given life through a relationship, and could expect to return to dust if that relationship did not continue.

The images of life in the New Testament do not come from a Greek idea of an innately immortal and divinely indestructible soul within man. They relate rather to new birth and resurrection. When Nicodemus encountered Jesus, as recorded in the third chapter of John, Jesus spoke of being born from above or being born anew. The belief focuses not on an indestructively divine substance called the soul surviving the destruction of the flesh, but on the dust and ashes of death from which a person will be born anew.

In the fifteenth chapter of 1 Corinthians Paul refers to the resurrection of the body as a renewal of life, a transition from fleshly limitations to spiritual power. Perhaps the best modern equivalent of the word "body" is person or personality. When Paul speaks of body, he does not mean flesh—indeed he speaks of bodies of flesh and bodies of spirit, as if they were quite distinct.

The development of Paul's thought in this respect is fascinating. In his earliest letter he wrote that believers who died were sleeping in their graves, and when Jesus Christ would come again they would rise from their graves at his appearing. Those who were alive would, together with those who had risen from the grave, be caught up in a rapturous mid-air reunion with Jesus Christ. (1 Thes. 4:14-17)

In his middle correspondence during the height of his career he begins to use the Resurrection of Jesus Christ as an analogy by which one might understand the Christian life. In speaking about the nature of the life of faith he said: "We were buried therefore with him by baptism in death, so that as Christ was raised from the dead by the glory of the Father, we too might walk in newness of life" (Rom. 6:4).

He goes on to speak of the Crucifixion of the "old self" which for Paul meant man's hostility to God. This death with Christ will be a prelude to resurrection with Christ or newness of life. In the passage from Romans he speaks about the death with Christ as a present reality, yet he also seems to indicate that the resurrection with Christ will be a future reality. He said that "we too might walk in newness of life . . . we shall be certainly united with him in a resurrection like his ... we shall also live with him" (Rom. 6:4-8).

There is a subtle shift of decisive importance in his last letters, written while he was in Rome awaiting his execution. In one of his prison Epistles, Colossians, he no longer uses such qualifiers as "might" and "shall." He says quite simply: "You were buried with him in baptism, in which you were also raised with him" (Col. 2:12). The verbal form of "raised" in Greek refers to a past action completed at a point in time, not some gradual process.

Thus the concept of resurrection changes from a futuristic doctrine related to the Second Coming of Jesus Christ to an analogy used to develop an understanding of the nature of the Christian life here and now. The meaning of death is no longer based on the concept of the dissolution of the physical body but now refers to the personal disintegration resulting from hostility to God. The resurrection is no longer the mere rising from graves but is now a newness of life lived not in hostility to God but in relationship with him in faith.

In Paul's later language death refers to a style of life. One dies to a life of achievement, and rises to a life of faith in God's graciousness. One dies to a self-justifying goodness and rises to a justified graciousness. Thus, the image of the resurrection comes to mean not only a life after death but also a life here and now.

The question of life after death is really a question of the quality of life here and now. If life is an achievement, a monument of goodness, then it will perish. The great issue in the Christian's belief in life after death is that life is not achievement, but a relationship with God. If he believes in life after death, he simply believes that God's relationship with him is stronger than the force of his own physical dissolution. The real question is the relative strengths of man and God. Is man's death stronger than God's relationship? The Resurrection of Jesus Christ was the answer to that question. God could survive the death of man's goodness.

Thus resurrection is but the beginning of life. As Paul developed the idea of resurrection, so John developed the idea of everlasting life. Paul welded the image of baptism to death and resurrection. By this analogy he illuminated the life of faith. The Christian's life was not his achievement but was God's gracious relationship with him in Jesus Christ.

In the prologue to the Gospel according to John it is said in referring to Jesus Christ: "To all who received him, who believed in his name, he gave power to become children of God; who were born, not of blood nor of the will of the flesh nor of the will of man, but of God" (John 1:12-13). This image of rebirth is developed throughout the rest of the Gospel.

The image of being born again or born from above comes out of the dialogue with Nicodemus. It is the first statement in the Gospel regarding how rebirth takes place. Nicodemus asks Jesus how a man can be born again, and Jesus replies that the Spirit moves where he wills. The import is that the new life is not an achievement but a gift of God. As with all gifts it cannot be earned or coerced. It comes on God's initiative.

The point is quite simple. Life is a matter of relationship. A man becomes alive not by anything he does but as a gift of the Holy Spirit. The gift is a relationship with God through Jesus Christ. The life is eternal or everlasting because it is a relationship with God who has endured and conquered man's death.

That is all quite different from a belief in the immortality of the soul, which posits life hereafter as a constituent part of man's being, his indestructible soul. For the biblical writers the emphasis is on God's gift. In the one instance man's hope is his strength; for Paul and John man's hope is in God's power.

The Greek point of view infected the Christian doctrines so thoroughly that one wonders if there will ever be a disengagement. The modern misinterpretation of the Christian faith generally hangs on two points. Some Christians believe, along with the Greeks, that man is inherently immortal. Others believe that one guarantees his everlasting state by his good deeds, his religiosity, or by the strength of his faith. However, for most people a belief in life after death is no longer a live issue. Indeed, even beer commercials stress the fact that a man only has one chance at life and had better enjoy it to the utmost while he can.

The modern disbelief in eternal life has a fairly solid foundation, for it has been well observed that the monuments of meaning do not endure. Indeed, one could even claim that the gradual erosion seen in modern, western culture of the old system of achievement is part of the reason for the modern disbelief in eternal life. The traditional values of western culture have been built upon a system of ethics rooted in achievement. Customarily this has been thought of as the province of capitalist cultures, but in their own way the communist societies are even more fiercely cultures of achievement.

Part of the revolt within western culture has been directed at its system of achievement; however, as in most revolts, the revolt is often just a house squabble. It assumes that which it is protesting against. Communism as a revolt against capitalism assumed more of capitalism than it repudiated. It assumed achievement. The modern revolts against communism and capitalism also assume achievement. The distinction is in the symbols of achievement. The work ethic has been replaced with the pleasure ethic. The compulsion to manufacture has been replaced with a compulsion to consume. The irony is that pleasure has become the measure of achievement, thus destroying pleasure; one cannot work at play.

Modern man has seen the destruction of so much he once thought permanent that it is small wonder he thinks life cannot endure death. Death has become his strongest experience, and, therefore, he cannot believe in life. Thinking that life after death is a belief rooted in a religious culture and finding himself in a supposedly secular culture, he has little reason to think of life eternal as either possible or pertinent.

The real question posed by the images of the resurrection of the body and the life everlasting is the nature and quality of life itself. Monuments die. They suffer the erosions of time and circumstance. As achievements neither manufacture nor consumption can last, and if one puts his faith in them it is small wonder that he believes in death; they are forms of death. Death is the attempt to live by achievement. It is hostility to God.

One of the arresting peculiarities of the Creed is its avoidance of any doctrine of hell, apart from the ref-

131

erence to Christ's descent into hell. Some people wonder about the completeness of the Creed since it leaves out any reference to the everlasting punishment of the wicked. Its silence reflects the silence of the New Testament, where the word "hell" occurs only once. The focus in the New Testament and in the Creed is on life, not punishment: God sent his son into the world, "not to condemn the world, but that the world might be saved through him" (John 5:17).

Within the thought of the New Testament the contrast is not essentially between heaven and hell as places of reward and punishment for good and bad lives. It is between life and death; according to John a man will die if he is not reborn. But the words are used in two ways. Death means, first of all, a ruinous existence on earth outside a relationship with God. Secondly, it means a final annihilation which would be the inevitable consummation of alienation from God. Paul develops the same idea with different imagery. Without the resurrection a man will live in hostility to God, and when he dies physically, he will be annihilated because of his alienation. So, death is used in two senses, one as a bare existence in estrangement from God and the other as a final annihilation. Neither view really has place for any everlasting torment.

In the synoptic Gospels of Matthew, Mark, and Luke, Jesus refers to the "fires of Gehenna," translated in the King James Version as the "fires of hell." However, Gehenna was not hell. It was a place a few miles southwest of Jerusalem which was used when the original inhabitants of the land sacrificed their first-born male children in fires to assure the continued fertility of their wives. During the time of Jesus it was used as a place where unclean refuse was burned; fires were kept burning there continually. As a place of abomination and desolation, Gehenna became a figure of speech used to indicate the ultimate in degradation. The notion was not everlasting punishment, but abomination. It was an image for death.

There is a third use of death in the New Testament. Paul speaks of dying to oneself. In the fifteenth chapter of 1 Corinthians he speaks of things dying that they may live, much as an ear of corn must die to produce seed so that it can generate life. John uses the image of a grain of wheat falling to the ground; it has to die to bear much fruit (John 12:24).

In this sense death is a form of life, or perhaps better, a prelude to life. It is the experience everyone has when everything has run out. As Jean Paul Sartre said, it is a "No Exit" sign placed at the end of man's hopes. This death is the realization that overcomes a man when he is just about to place the finishing touches on the monument to his life's meaning and finds that the foundation is beginning to give way. It is the death that comes to a man when he becomes aware that he has missed the point of life, that he has striven mightily, achieved much, and gone nowhere. When that experience of death overtakes a person, when he gives up on the achievement of goodness and responds instead to God's offer of graciousness, then the person has undergone a death, a death that is indeed a prelude to life.

The resurrection of the body and the life everlasting point two ways, to now and to then, to the quality of a man's life in the here and now and to the continuation of that life beyond the bounds of vision. In effect, his belief in life after death says something of his belief about life in the here and now.

If one does not believe in life after death, he in effect believes that death is stronger than life; he has defined his life in terms of death and understood it as a fading monument. Some who believe in life after death live the illusion that they are indestructible or can fashion something indestructible. Both views fly in the face of the facts. They are absurdities. Yet one can still believe that his life is the gift of a relationship and that relationships are stronger than the death of his monuments of meaning.

A belief in everlasting life and the resurrection of the body is a question about life. Is it an accomplishment or is it a gift? If life is an accomplishment of man, then death prevails. If it is a gift of God, then life prevails.